V-WEAPONS
BOMBER COMMAND
FAILED TO RETURN

Published in 2015 by Fighting High Ltd
www.fightinghigh.com

British Library Cataloguing-in-Publication data. A CIP record
for this title is available from the British Library.

ISBN 978 0 9926207 9 0

Designed by www.truthstudio.co.uk.
Printed and bound in China by Toppan Leefung.

To Colin

Geo Dunn DFC
10 76 608 1409 Mel Flt

Dave Fellowes
460 Sqn
RAAF.

V-WEAPONS
BOMBER COMMAND

**FAILED TO
RETURN**

STEVE BOND, STEVE DARLOW, SEAN FEAST, MARC HALL, ROBERT OWEN
AND HOWARD SANDALL

FH

CONTENTS

72

78

100

28

42

50 12

110

88

62

14

FOREWORD

BY FLIGHT LIEUTENANT GEORGE DUNN DFC

George Dunn completed forty-four operations flying as a pilot with RAF Bomber Command, serving with Nos 10 and 76 Squadrons on Handley Page Halifaxes, and 608 Squadron and 1409 Met Flight on De Havilland Mosquitoes. In 1943, while serving with No. 76 Squadron, George took part in Operation 'Hydra', the all-out attack on the German secret weapon research establishment at Peenemünde on the Baltic coast.

O N THE NIGHT of 17/18 August 1943 Bomber Command undertook one of the most important raids of the war. It was on a previously unknown target, but so important to the safety of this country that the commander-in-chief of Bomber Command, Sir Arthur Harris, ordered a maximum effort and 596 bombers were sent. We were not told the precise nature of the work being carried out at the target, other than it was radar connected and that it must be destroyed that night – if we did not succeed, the bombers would have to go back the following night, and every night, until a satisfactory result was obtained. I am sure that an order such as this was never issued on any other occasion. The crews set off with this sombre thought on their minds, knowing the sort of reception that would be waiting if they were indeed forced to return the following night.

The target was Peenemünde on the Baltic coast, about 100 miles north of Berlin and, as we found out much later, an experimental establishment for the production of the V1 flying bomb and the V2 rocket. My flight engineer, Sergeant Ferris Newton, kept a diary while flying with me at No. 76 Squadron and recorded how the night unfolded for us. The day before we had taken on a new aircraft, rather suitably lettered 'G' for George. Ferris wrote:

Took her on a fuel consumption test, over Tunstall and the low flying area. Had a few minutes hedge hopping.

The 17th of August was a bad day for the Germans. Butch Harris ... had decided to send a large force of his slaves to bomb the secret weapon base at Peenemünde, situated 60 miles N.W. of Stettin on the Baltic coast. ... Our aiming point was on the staff blocks and living quarters for the professors. We were told at briefing by

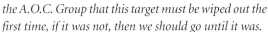

the A.O.C. Group that this target must be wiped out the first time, if it was not, then we should go until it was.

It was a beautiful night, with a very bright moon and the target was not very well defended with flak. But when Jerrie [sic] found out where the raid was actually taking place he sent up a host of night fighters. We bombed from 7,000 feet, almost low level for us chaps, and we were in the first wave in, so we were clear of the target when most of the Jerrie fighters appeared. We had been routed as for Berlin but we turned smartly to port dropping low over Peenemünde, so of course Jerrie was late in concentrating his forces there. He had held them for the defence of Berlin, just as we had been told he would do. … Crews going in on the later waves said the sky was full of fighters. Nothing like being first there, catch 'em when they are asleep.

We were indeed fortunate that night. The raid was a success on the first sortie, much to the relief of the surviving crews, but the grim total of 40 bombers had failed to return, with 243 airmen killed and 45 becoming prisoners of war. Their sacrifice, however, greatly delayed the German long-range weapon assault on this island of ours and saved the lives of several thousand civilians. General Dwight D. Eisenhower in his book *Crusade in Europe* was of the opinion that the second front would have been seriously compromised had the Germans been able to use the V2 rocket earlier.

Our raid against the research station at Peenemünde was the first major counter-attack against the V-weapon threat, and in 1944 when the V1s and V2s began to kill and destroy indiscriminately in southern England, my Bomber Command colleagues once more took it upon themselves to seek out and attack the whole V-weapon launch and supply system. History now shows that they were able to diminish the scale of the assault on us, and save civilian lives, but many had done so at the cost of their own.

In this book you will find a selection of stories telling of Bomber Command airmen who fought in the direct defence of this country, against Hitler's 'reprisal weapons', and in doing so paid with their lives, or just their short-term freedom, as POWs, if they were lucky. In recent years the scale of loss suffered by the aircrews of Bomber Command during the Second World War has finally received long-overdue international recognition. Within that context the story of those killed defending against the V-weapons deserves to be told. 'We Will Remember Them.'

INTRODUCTION

BY STEVE DARLOW

T HE ENEMY WAS up to something. And it was clearly something sinister that could change the course of the Second World War. The Allies watched and listened as intelligence from agents and reconnaissance accumulated, and it steadily became apparent that the Nazi regime was developing a highly dangerous secret weapon programme – preparing and threatening an unprecedented all-out assault upon the British population.

In the summer of 1944 the threat became a reality as Hitler launched his terrifying Vergeltungswaffen (reprisal weapons) against the population of southeast England. Under direct attack the Allies responded. Somehow they had to limit the scale of the attack – to protect the civilian population and maintain the momentum in Normandy following the D-Day landings. On the night of 15/16 June the V1 offensive had opened in earnest with an estimated 300 flying bombs launched by the Germans in the next twenty-four hours, 144 reaching English skies and 73 striking London, causing death and destruction. The Supreme Allied Commander, General Dwight D. Eisenhower, was clear when he stated on 16 June that with respect to V-weapon targets they were 'to take first priority over everything except the urgent requirements of the [land] battle; this priority to obtain until we can be certain that we have definitely gotten the upper hand of this particular business'. He would use all the resources at his disposal, including the Royal Air Force's heavy bomber force.

RAF Bomber Command had already been in action against V-weapon targets, starting with the August 1943 successful attack on the German research station at Peenemünde – but at the cost of forty aircraft and crew. Then as Allied intelligence went on to identify V-weapon launch sites and storage facilities in northern France, Bomber Command was tasked with their obliteration. When the first V1 flying bombs crashed to earth on English soil in June 1944 the Allied command were quick to launch defensive and counter-offensive measures. The task for RAF Bomber Command was simple: if the bomber crews could reduce the number of V1s launched, the fighter aircraft and gun defences had a better chance to intercept and shoot down the flying bombs that did come over. But the flying bomb was not the only menace; the V2 rocket offensive would soon commence, and the Allies also closely monitored the construction of what they came to learn was the V3 'super-gun' site.

When the war came to a close Bomber Command

Clockwise from left
A V1 flying bomb;
A V2 rocket launch.
Fighting High

A Handley Page
Halifax is silhouetted
against target
indicators descending
over the target during
the bombing of a V1
flying bomb storage
dump at Biennais,
France, at 3.38 am
on 6 July 1944.

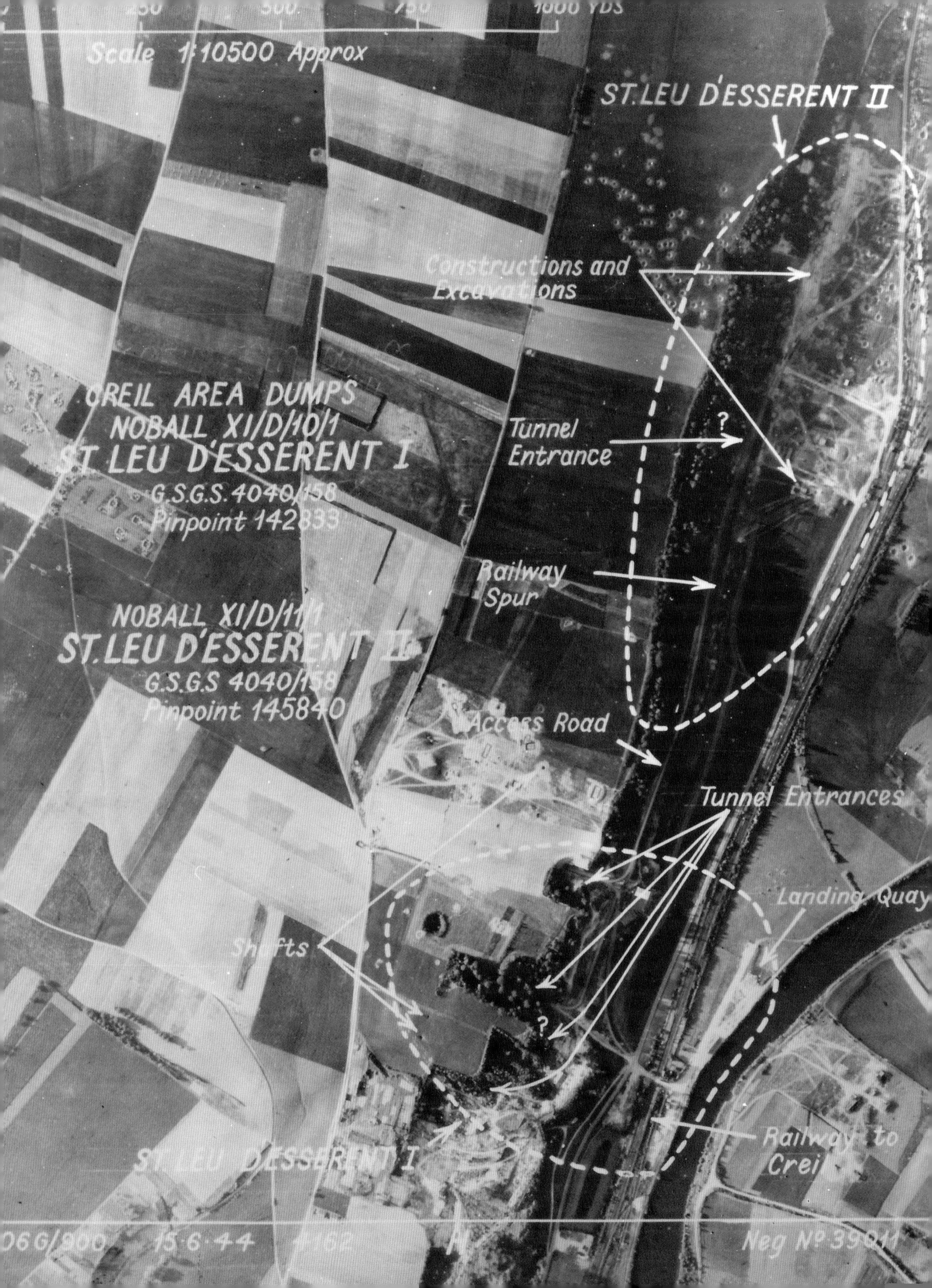

250   500   750   1000 YDS

Scale 1:10500 Approx

ST. LEU D'ESSERENT II

Constructions and
Excavations

CREIL AREA DUMPS
NOBALL XI/D/10/1
ST LEU D'ESSERENT I
G.S.G.S. 4040/158
Pinpoint 142833

Tunnel
Entrance

?

NOBALL XI/D/11/1
ST. LEU D'ESSERENT II
G.S.G.S 4040/158
Pinpoint 145840

Railway
Spur

Access Road

Tunnel Entrances

Landing Quay

Shafts

?

ST. LEU D'ESSERENT I

Railway to
Creil

06 G/900   15.6.44   162   Neg N° 39011

Previous page 10-11
The bombing of the underground caves at St Leu D'Esserent was one of the most effective counter measures against the German flying bomb offensive. The site was used for the storage of V1s prior to distribution to launch sites. The annotated photograph on the left, taken on 15 June 1944, shows how much the Allies knew of the layout of the area. The photograph on the right, taken after the Bomber Command attack of 7/8 July 1944, reveals the extent of the bombing, which seriously disrupted the German V1 supply system, thus lowering the scale of attack.

Right A V1 'ski' site under attack. Note the 'ski' shaped constructions where the flying bombs were stored; The V1 'ski' site at Bois Des Huits Rues
Fighting High

could justifiably claim success against the V-weapons. The Command had made a sizeable commitment to 'Crossbow' (the codeword for Allied operations against all aspects of the German long-range weapon programme). A greater tonnage of bombs was dropped by Bomber Command on Crossbow targets than on all targets during the year 1942, and larger than that dropped on Berlin in the entire war. The number of V1s launched had been very much reduced, the V2 rocket offensive had been considerably delayed – the British official history of the war claiming by at least two months – and the V3 silenced by bombing before a shot was fired. Lord Cherwell, scientific adviser to Winston Churchill, reported in April 1945: 'If the Germans had not been interfered with, they would have been able to launch 300 [V1s] a day – or more if they had drawn on stocks. 200 or more would have crossed the coast instead of 68. I do not know whether with this greater concentration we

could have brought down such a large proportion; even if we had done, London would have received over three times what it actually did.'

There was a cost, though – a cost in aircrew lives. In the period from the Peenemünde raid until 3 September 1944 a total of 253 Bomber Command aircraft were lost. On raids to V-weapon targets specifically in France, just over 1,000 aircrew failed to return, and three-quarters of these men now rest in French cemeteries or are listed as missing.

V-Weapons Bomber Command – Failed to Return tells the story of some of those airmen who were prepared to risk their lives countering the German V-weapon offensive in direct defence of the civilian population. They, along with thousands of their fellow airmen, had responded to what British Prime Minister Winston Churchill described as the attempt to 'blast the viper in his nest'.

Left A damaged V1 launch ramp photographed after the Allies had liberated northern France. *Fighting High*

CHAPTER ONE

A MATTER OF TIME

BY HOWARD SANDALL

IN 2006 IN THE NORTHERN FRENCH VILLAGE OF SOCX, A HOUSING COMPLEX WAS NAMED IN HONOUR OF TWO SECOND WORLD WAR AIRCREW MEMBERS TRAGICALLY KILLED ON THEIR FIRST OPERATION. THE FRENCH POPULATION OF SOCX HAD NOT FORGOTTEN THEIR SACRIFICE. FAMILY, FRIENDS AND DIGNITARIES GATHERED IN THIS SMALL VILLAGE TO WITNESS THE CEREMONY IN HONOUR OF THE TWO DEAD SERVICE-MEN, SIXTY-TWO YEARS AFTER THEIR LANCASTER BOMBER CRASHED NEAR THEIR VILLAGE. THE NAMING OF THE NEW HOUSING COMPLEX 'RUE F. OLIVER ET W.H. COOKE' WILL BE A LASTING TESTIMONY TO FREDERICK OLIVER, RAF, AND WILFRED HAROLD COOKE, RNZAF. THE TWO AIRMEN EPITOMISE THE BONDS OF FRIENDSHIP THAT SPREAD OUT FROM ALL CORNERS OF THE COMMONWEALTH. THE PILOT, A NEW ZEALANDER, THE AIR GUNNER AN ENGLISHMAN, LIE SIDE BY SIDE IN DEATH AS THEY STOOD SHOULDER TO SHOULDER IN LIFE. THEIR TARGET WAS A V1 LAUNCHING SITE AT L'HEY IN NORTHERN FRANCE AND A NEW FORM OF 'TERROR WEAPON' THAT HAD BEGUN RAINING DOWN DEATH INDISCRIMINATELY ON ITS VICTIMS JUST A WEEK BEFORE.

THE TIDE WAS TURNING against Adolf Hitler and Germany. D-Day on 6 June 1944 had been a relative success and the Germans were on the defensive; most with a sense of foresight understood that inevitable defeat would only be a matter of time. British intelligence had known for some while that Hitler placed great faith in the development of rockets or V1s, his Vergeltungswaffe, meaning retaliation weapon. The pilotless, flying bombs carried a significant amount of explosives and could be launched from ramps in the Pas de Calais area of northern France.

On 13 June 1944, the first of the V1 flying bombs were launched against London. Air Chief Marshal Sir Arthur Harris, Bomber Command's commander-in-chief, was fully committed to bombing targets in support of the Allied invasion. The flying bomb objective became a priority when the Germans launched their flying bomb campaign, raining V1 rockets down on the inhabitants of London and the Home Counties until late into August. The codeword for attacks against V-weapons was 'Crossbow.' Across all commands 443 Allied aircraft were lost, along with 2,924 airmen, against these targets.

No. 622 Squadron Lancaster LM138, piloted by

Left Harold Cooke
Courtesy of K. Oliver

Warrant Officer Wilfred Harold Cooke, RNZAF, would be among the loss statistics. This chapter relays the personal story of this particular crew and the families' anguish.

Left Frederick Oliver
Courtesy of K. Oliver

Sixty-two years after the fateful night of 23/24 June 1944, Kathleen Oliver, in a quiet moment of reflection, stood by the graveside of her husband Frederick and his pilot Wilfred Harold Cooke. Her journey to be here had taken over six decades and a lot of soul-searching. With her family by her side, it was time to draw some solace from a lifetime's emotions.

The French community felt it appropriate to name the housing complex in their honour. The civilians who witnessed the dramatic events in the early hours of 24 June 1944, still held the emotional scars. Kathleen and her family were able to visit the crash site in a farmer's field. A propeller from the Lancaster still rests next to a farm building, its twisted and buckled blades stand as an unofficial memorial. A simple touch of this inanimate object provides a link to the past.

The years had not diminished Kathleen's love and sense of loss. Fred had been torn away from her – one moment she was blissfully happy, the next sadly widowed. They had only been married for four months when the 'Missing in Action' telegram arrived

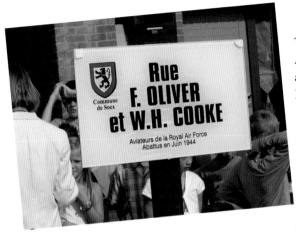

Right The housing complex in Socx village northern France. Opened in 2006 to commemorate the sad demise of Frederick Oliver and Wilfred Cooke. *Courtesy of K. Oliver*

unexpectedly. At the time of his death she was pregnant with his son.

Frederick Oliver was born in Wigan, Lancashire, on 14 November 1921, the eldest of four children to John and Mary. His father had seen active service in the First World War and died in 1937 from decompression sickness, commonly known as the 'bends', while constructing a tunnel. Fifteen-year-old Frederick became head of the household and he matured quickly. His childhood was indicative of the period, making his own entertainment among his peers in the back streets of an industrial town.

On 22 February 1944, the Church of the Sacred Heart in Wigan was full to capacity for the wedding of Frederick Oliver and Kathleen Lowe. The best man was Kathleen's brother, James, a serving soldier who saw action in Africa. The couple were very much in love. Marriage during wartime was a huge risk, especially for aircrew in having the highest attrition rate of any armed service.

Right Fredrick and Kathleen Oliver on their wedding day, four months before he was KIA. *Courtesy of K. Oliver*

Frederick originally joined the RAF as a mechanic, later volunteering for aircrew and specialising in air gunnery training. His training record is unclear. However, he would have followed the same course of tuition as other aircrew at the time. Firstly, by joining an Initial Training Wing (ITW), usually at a seaside town, for six weeks. From there he would have been sent to an Air Gunnery School for six months. Eventually he was transferred to No. 11 Operational Training Unit (OTU) at RAF Westcott where he 'crewed up'. The airmen gathered and formed into aircrews. How he came to join the 'Cooke' crew is unclear – usually this was based on first impressions or having prior knowledge of another airman and being invited to join a crew.

Wilfred Harold Cooke was born on 29 July 1919 in Te Awamutu, in New Zealand's North Island. He Attended Manurwa public school and left to become a cattle herd tester working for the Auckland Herd Improvement Association. The call to arms was especially strong for the Commonwealth countries, feeling both an obligation and a sense of patriotism, in equal measures. Young men and women felt it their duty to fight in defence of their King. Wilfred was of the same opinion: he wanted to fight the aggressors dealing out tyranny and cruelty to the free world. In January 1942 he commenced pilot training at No. 1 Elementary Flying Training School (EFTS) at Taieri, Dunedin, on South Island. Instruction included flights in de Havilland DH82a Tiger Moths, combined with intensive classroom theory. The Canadian contribution towards the Commonwealth Air Training Plan was to train pilots, navigators and bomb aimers in large numbers. Wilfred Cooke sailed on 10 May 1942, destined for Canada, where he arrived on 1 June and was assigned to No. 37 Standard Flight Training School (SFTS) at McCall Field, Calgary. The course content included the theory of flight, combined with navigation and flying at the controls of twin-engine

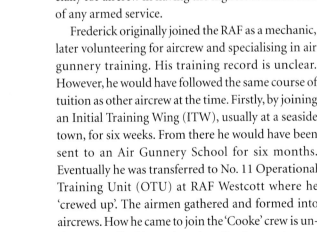

Avro Ansons and Cessna Cranes. The candidates had to fly solo and achieve high marks in the navigational elements to pass successfully the final assessment. On 25 September Wilfred was awarded his pilot's wings and sergeant's stripes in recognition of his accomplishment.

On 28 September he boarded a ship destined for Great Britain, arriving on these shores on 5 November. His subsequent journey through training is a familiar route for aircrew destined for Bomber Command:

• 28 December 1942:
  No. 15 Advanced Flying School (AFS).
• 9–15 February 1943:
  No. 1 Blind Approach School (BAS). Flying and landing on instruments using wireless operation and navigational skills. Assistance from air traffic control.
• 23 March–11 June 1943:
  Hospitalised, cause unknown.
• 27 June–1 July 1943: No. 1 Blind Approach School (BAS).
• 3–9 August 1943:
  No. 11 Operational Training Unit (OTU) based at RAF Westcott, flying Vickers Wellington bombers as a bomber crew.
• 21 September 1943:
  No. 1653 Heavy Conversion Unit based at RAF Chedburgh. Introduction to four-engine bombers, in this case the Short Stirling. Undertook familiarisation flights, circuits and landings, Cross-country exercises to test navigation and wireless operator efficiency.
• 14 April 1944:
  No. 3 Lancaster Finishing School based at RAF Feltwell; first opportunity to fly the Avro Lancaster and prepare to take it to war.
• 24 May 1944: No. 622 Squadron, part of 3 Group Bomber Command based at RAF Mildenhall in Suffolk.

By early May 1944 the crew had completed months of aircrew training and were informed that they were ready to commence operational flying with a front-line bomber squadron. They reported to the main gate at RAF Mildenhall on 24 May to join No. 622 Squadron, part of 3 Group Bomber Command. The crew

who arrived for operational duty comprised the following:

Pilot: Flight Sergeant Wilfred Harold Cooke (later Warrant Officer), RNZAF, from Te Awamutu, New Zealand.
Navigator: Flight Sergeant Ronald James Hansford, RAF, from East Ham, London.
Bomb aimer: Flight Sergeant R.J. Chapman, RAAF.
Wireless operator: Flying Officer Albert William Simmonds, RAF, from Langham, Holt, Norfolk.
Mid-upper gunner: Sergeant Frederick Oliver, RAF, from Beech Hill, Wigan, Lancashire.
Rear gunner: Flight Sergeant Thirlstane Durrant, RNZAF, from Auckland, New Zealand.
Flight engineer: Sergeant Donald Meese, RAF, from Norwood, Sheffield, Yorkshire.

RAF Mildenhall was a pre-war base and home to Nos 15 and 622 Squadrons. Aircrews were provided the luxury of houses as opposed to the usual hastily built billets. The crew's arrival coincided with the final preparations for the D-day landings on 6 June and attacks against the German oil industry by night.

Left Wilfred Harold Cooke RNZAF. Photo taken in the spring of 1944 in the Suffolk Countryside.
Courtesy of K.Oliver

Right Crew photograph taken shortly after arrival at RAF Mildenhall in May 1944. The black cat in the arms of F/Sgt Durrant is a reminder of how luck, good or bad, played a significant part in survival. Crew standing L-R: F/Sgt Cooke RNZAF, F/O Simmonds, F/Sgt Chapman RAAF, F/Sgt Hansford. Front L-R: F/Sgt Durrant RNZAF, Sgt Oliver. *Courtesy of K. Oliver.*

By far the most supporting role for the invasion by Bomber Command was that against military positions in the invasion area. Bomber Command's resources would be further stretched with the continuing destruction of railway, communication and oil targets in support of the advancing Allied armies.

The first few days involved more intensive training, including fighter affiliation exercises and loaded climbs with dummy bombs being dropped into the North Sea. Classroom lectures continued, with the essential repetitive escape and evasion lecture. New crews were often deployed to assist with test flights on the aircraft they were destined to fly on operations that night. If a crew were on the battle order they would test fly the Lancaster that was assigned to them, thoroughly checking the navigational aids, guns, radio, electrics and hydraulic systems. Any faults were reported to the ground crew, who worked incredibly hard to keep the aircraft fit for flight.

Unbeknown to the aircrew their activities were being monitored by the flight commander who was assessing them for operational readiness. After one month the crew were considered prepared to commence sorties against the enemy. Before the crew became operational as a unit, Flight Sergeant Cooke completed a 'second dickey' trip with an experienced pilot. On the night of 17/18 June the battle order was promulgated, with Lancaster R5514, GI-V, assigned to Flight Sergeant C. Fenwick, carrying Cooke on an operation to bomb a target at Montdidier. The crews took off at 00:55 hours and reached the target only for the 'master bomber' to cancel the operation due to 10/10ths cloud cover. They arrived back at RAF Mildenhall at 05:15 hours, disappointed this would not count towards their 'tour' of operations.

A barrage of questions ensued from Cooke's own crew, all eager to know how it felt. On 23 June the crew found themselves listed on the battle order, although at this stage they did not know the target; that would be revealed later during the main briefing. The Lancaster allocated to them on this occasion displayed the squadron markings of GI-N, serial No. LM138. A

Left and following page Although degraded over time two photographs exist that were taken at the crash scene by the Germans. A French local was asked to develop the pictures and secretly kept a copy for himself. On this and the next page the scenes show the German Luftwaffe guards surveying the mangled burned out wreckage at dawn. *From the original source of André Berteloot via K. Oliver.*

twenty-five minute test flight unsurprisingly revealed no problems; the Lancaster had only arrived on the squadron on 20 May with just thirty-three hours' flying time. A point of historical interest can be drawn from the Lancaster that previously bore the same squadron codes, LM108, which had become part of the squadron on the same day. Shot down on its first operation to Angers on the night of 28/29 May 1944, the pilot, Flight Sergeant T.R. Teague, RNZAF, was taken as a prisoner of war along with four of his crew; the remaining two evaded capture and were returned to England with the assistance of the French resistance movement.

The ground crew waited at the dispersal point for reported faults with the Lancaster. Cooke cut power to the four Rolls-Royce Merlin Type 24 engines and silence enveloped the cockpit. Sergeant Meese was standing beside him checking the dials and systems associated with his role as flight engineer. The silence brought a moment of clarity and realisation of what would happen next – it would be for real, and the

enemy would be shooting at them. The ground staff of each aircraft had a massive task in preparing the Lancaster for the operation, including fitting the bomb load, ammunition and fuel load. Each ground crew member was highly trained in his respective role and all gained the respect of airmen, for they toiled in all weathers on an open airfield to help keep their crews safe in the air.

It had been a pleasant early summer's day at Mildenhall; the sun shone on the ground crew, working in comfortable heat with their shirts removed. What a difference to the extreme cold endured throughout the winter months, the finger-numbing activities of touching metal in sub-zero temperatures now a distant memory. As dusk arrived thoughts turned towards the task ahead; as take-off time approached the tension on the station became almost palpable.

Ninety-eight aircrew from No. 622 Squadron, equating to fourteen crews, were among the airmen from No. 15 Squadron waiting anxiously in the spacious briefing room. The conversation would reverberate around the room, raising the decibels in a crescendo of sound. The large door at the back of the room opened and in an instant the noise abated, and all gathered there stood to attention as a mark of respect. The revered commanding officers from both squadrons walked in, closely followed by flight commanders, senior leaders in navigation, bombing, wireless operation, flight engineering and gunnery. Perhaps the most notable presentation to the assembled mass was the meteorological officer. He would report on the projected weather to the target, over the target and return journey. The large map of Europe on the back wall was shrouded with a curtain; beneath, the target route was plotted with a silk cord marking the point at which the aircraft would leave the English coast to the all-important target point. On this occasion the target was revealed to be a flying bomb site at L'Hey, within the Pas de Calais region.

The crew were understandably anxious prior to their first operation, that would put them in harm's way. Targets in France were considered as 'easy trips' by experienced bomber crews; it was less distance to travel, avoiding the Ruhr valley defences, which thereby increased the chance of survival. In reality, there were no 'easy targets'; the German night-fighter force was formidable, choosing their victims indiscriminately, vectoring on to a guided target by their radar control station. The rest was dependent upon on-board radar named 'Lichtenstein', abbreviated to SN2. The system was very efficient, developed in response to the radar countermeasures deployed by Bomber Command.

Shortly before take-off Cooke taxied LM138, GI-N from its dispersal point snaking from right to left, his confident handling of the large bomber an assurance to his crew. Accelerating to 110 mph down the runway Cooke pulled back on the control column, accepting responsibility for all on board. The aircraft struggled into the air, the creaking airframe and slow rate of climb an indication that they were fully laden with bombs, fuel and seven crew members. In the

houses and cottages of the Suffolk town of Mildenhall below, the familiar sound of the bombers clawing into the night sky always brought a moment of contemplation and prayer. After the noise followed silence.

The bombers crossed the coast at Bradwell Bay. Beyond the English Channel, the target objective of L'Hey was a small hamlet just a few hundred metres from Noordpeene village in northern France. Sergeant Meese set the propellers to coarse pitch, matching the rate of climb and to conserve fuel. Six tanks of fuel in each wing had to be balanced to assist the flight and trimming of the aircraft. In addition he monitored the mass of gauges to reflect engine rpm, indicated air speed, fuel usage, oil pressure and temperature. Twenty-minute observations were recorded on a Flight Engineer's Log (form BC/F7), which would be assessed by the flight engineer 'leader' during the post operation debrief.

Approaching the target, the red pathfinder target flares dropped by de Havilland Mosquitoes were clear to see. Flight Sergeant Chapman, RAAF, released the bombs from a height of approximately 7,500 feet. With a massive sense of relief, Cooke put the Lancaster's nose down and dived out of the target area while asking navigator, Flight Sergeant Hansford, for a course to steer. Peering into the night sky both gunners knew more than anyone that they were still vulnerable. Cocooned in the rear turret, Thirlstane Durrant of the Royal New Zealand Air Force could be forgiven for his nervous tension, his thoughts playing through every possible scenario. Suddenly, out of the gloom the silhouette of a Ju88 night fighter appeared. Aware of the imminent danger he called 'corkscrew port' over the intercom, simultaneously to the flashes of 20mm cannon fire that tore into the fuselage and port wing. The aircraft shuddered under the impact; exploding shells exhibited the smell of cordite inside the aircraft. In an instant, the lives of all on board had dramatically changed. It now became a battle for survival.

At the controls, Cooke struggled to pull the Lancaster out of the corkscrew manoeuvre; it became obvious that they were doomed as the controls gave limited response and the fuel tanks in the port wing became a blazing inferno, spreading flames down the fuselage. Fear and confusion overwhelmed the crew. Could this really be happening to them on their first operation? The stark reality of their predicament

Left Donald Meese.
Courtesy of C. Meese

pumped the adrenaline, heightening their instinct for survival. Sergeant Meese frantically tried to extinguish the flames in the wing, but he knew that the crew only had a few seconds to get out before the aircraft exploded.

Having retreated to a safe distance in the dark, Unteroffizier Konrad Beyer from 1./NJG4 based at Florennes in France, knew he had dealt the bomber a fatal blow. The flaming wing could be seen lighting the night sky like a beacon. He made a mental note of the time – twenty-eight minutes past midnight, point south of Calais, kill number seven. By the end of the war Beyer would add four more bombers to his tally and he was bestowed the accolade of 'ace'.

Information filtered through that Sergeant Oliver had been hit and was unresponsive in the mid-upper turret. Cooke was in a dilemma and his decision had fatal consequences. He reluctantly gave the order to bale out. Chapman, in the bomb-aimer's position pulled open the escape hatch directly underneath him and dropped into the night sky. Donald Meese quickly passed his skipper his parachute and followed the bomb aimer out of the front hatch. Five of the crew parachuted into the dark. Two of their colleagues remained in the bomber.

The hopes and dreams of Wilfred Cooke and Frederick Oliver lay scattered on the ground. Their lives once interwoven were now in pieces for all to see. The crash was heard by the local community, including local farmer Paul Vandaele and his wife. Intrigued, they went to see if they could help in any way. The scene that confronted them was unimaginable: a burning pyre raged among a mass of crumpled metal. Several parts of the aircraft could be distinguished, such as the engine, propellers and the cockpit, identifiable from the flames reflecting against the smashed Perspex. Ammunition exploded due to the heat and the German soldiers cordoned off the area. Standing in the shadows was eighteen-year-old Andre Berteloot. He witnessed the horror and reality of war.

Research revealed that Wilfred Cooke attempted to land the Lancaster in a field, unsure if Fred Oliver was alive or not in the mid-upper turret. This selfless act took his life; he was removed from behind the aircraft controls the next day by Monsieur Roger Caillau, a local carpenter. Under instruction from the Germans he made the two coffins in which he laid to rest the fallen aircrew.

Sergeant Donald Meese's story is remarkable, borne out of compassion and a sense of duty, and his time in captivity would be eventful. On his return to Britain the whole country had the opportunity to hear about his exploits when they were made into a feature film.

Born on 2 May 1923 in Norwood, Sheffield, Donald was the younger of two boys. His father Walter Meese had been a soldier in the First World War and like so many had been gassed on the front lines. It deeply affected his son. One day he sent Donald (aged five) and his brother Walter (aged nine) to buy him some cigarettes from the local shop. On their return they found their father dead from gas inhalation.

Donald left grammar school at the age of fourteen to work as a pageboy at the prestigious Victoria Station Hotel, followed by a brief period at Timpsons shoe shop. His final job prior to joining the RAF was at the steel rolling mills. The Luftwaffe bombed the mills and shortly afterwards two members of the RAF visited the factory to thank all the workers for their contribution towards the war effort. Donald instantly made his mind up to join the RAF and wreak revenge

Right Donald Meese's POW identity card produced whilst he was held captive in Stalag Luft 7.
Courtesy of C. Meese

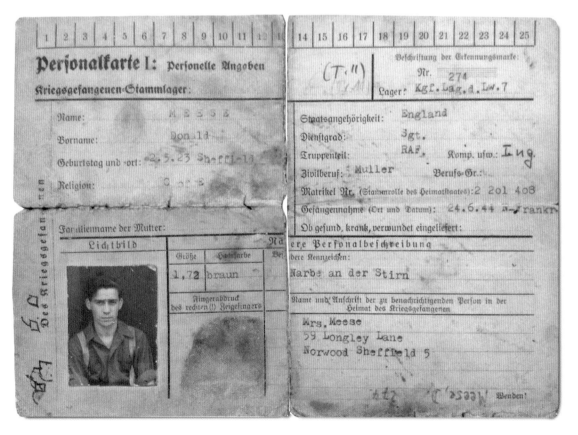

on the enemy. Being in a reserved occupation brought the challenge of being accepted; however, he was determined to win the two packets of cigarettes bet by his foreman if he was successful.

He was finally given the opportunity to undertake flight engineer training; his aptitude tests reflected a particular strength in this discipline. Training commenced with a posting to an Initial Training Wing (ITW) at Torquay in Devon. This was his introduction to RAF life with discipline, fitness and basic understanding of Morse code part of the course. From here he was posted for trade training at RAF St Athan in Wales, a six-month course concentrating on mechanical and electrical components. He passed out with an above average grade and moved to an Operational Training Unit where he 'crewed up' and originally joined No. 620 Squadron at RAF Chedburgh, completing twelve operations.

Returning to the fateful night of 23/24 June, Donald Meese fell through the night air, the noisy Merlin engines still ringing in his ears in stark contrast to the eerie silence thrust upon him as he descended. The parachute webbing caught the side of his face as it opened – the jolt breaking his fall abruptly and painfully. As he tumbled under his parachute canopy a moment of clarity consumed him; he could see the burning Lancaster falling to earth in the distance and he hoped all the crew had managed to escape. Hitting the ground hard took his breath away and he was briefly dragged across the ground with the wind-filled canopy. All the lectures on escape and evasion proved useful as he buried his parachute, turned his jacket inside out and cut his flying boots down. Lying in a cornfield to collect his thoughts made him realise that he would be leaving a trail of trampled-down corn, allowing the Germans to track him.

He decided to walk alongside the hedgerows and at dawn he came across a church where he met up with four Frenchmen. The fear of being caught harbouring or assisting shot-down aircrew was ever present; the French had witnessed the consequences of such actions. The civilians pointed him in the right direction and Donald continued to use the hedges as cover, until his luck ran out. Four German soldiers emerged from the hedgerow behind him and tapped him on the shoulder. He became a prisoner of war and was taken to a large castle where he met up with surviving members of his crew. Shortly after being offered some

coffee and a meal, he was taken to the crash site and had the unenviable task of identifying the bodies of his pilot and mid-upper gunner. The crew eventually found themselves incarcerated at Lille prison, where they were subjected to solitary confinement, interrogation and psychological torture by the Gestapo. It was while at Lille that he experienced some compassion when a young German guard shared his food and cigarettes with each of them.

Left Donald and Ursula welcomed by his mother and niece on arrival back in England.
Courtesy of C. Meese

Five days later Donald and the rest of the crew were transported to different prisoner of war camps. He was sent to Stalag Luft 7 in Bankau, Upper Silesia, then in Germany and now a part of Poland. The camp held around 230 prisoners. Life was tedious and Donald was keen to escape at the first opportunity. He focused his attentions on keeping fit and struck up a friendship with a Dutchman. Both were determined to make a break for it. Every day Donald and his companion would run around the perimeter of the camp improving their fitness in readiness for their bid for freedom.

In late 1944, a chance meeting would change his life forever and be immortalised in a film. Eighteen-year-old English-speaking nurse Ursula Maria Mosler was sent to work in the camp. She refused to assist the Germans, not believing in their Nazi party rhetoric. Her punishment was to work at the camp undertaking menial tasks. Donald struck up a friendship with Ursula and became very fond of her.

On 19 January 1945, the prisoners were ordered to pack up and leave. The Russians were advancing from the east and the enemy was afraid that any POWs left behind would join the fight against them. Subsequently the entire camp would be marched on foot

Right The telegram received by Kathleen informing her that Frederick was 'missing from air operations.
Courtesy of C. Meese

across 650 miles of inhospitable territory in sub-zero temperatures; the intended destination was Stalag Luft IIIA near Luckenwalde, a place deeper into Germany. The prisoners were desperately short of food and warm clothing. Weak from years in a POW camp, many had malnutrition and dysentery from eating rotten food and no healthcare. They sheltered where they could, more often than not in barns that offered a welcome respite from the bitter wind and snow. Those who could not keep up the pace were left behind or, if lucky, thrown on to horse-drawn carts for the journey. At this time Donald's fitness paid dividends. He watched the guards patrolling the line of prisoners and calculated a sixteen-second opportunity to escape. When the column of men were rested at a brickworks, Donald and his Dutch friend hid behind a wood pile and seized the moment, running for their lives towards the distant forest. They were now alone, cold and hungry in a strange country surrounded by fighting forces. They navigated their way by the night stars and spent eight days walking in the bitterly cold conditions, taking cover where they could huddle together for warmth. While sheltering in a barn they were disturbed by a young girl. With practically impossible odds, the young woman was Ursula Mosler, the same girl Donald had befriended in Stalag Luft 7. Both were surprised to see each other

and she gave them bread and boiled eggs to eat. Eventually the pair ran into Russian soldiers, who took some convincing that they were Allied escapees. But they believed their story and treated them well. They were passed back down the Russian lines, reaching Częstochowa in southern Poland. Donald met up with Ursula once again. He was well aware that her life would be uncertain under Russian rule and he was determined to repay her kindness to him. They both agreed to a marriage of convenience to allow Donald to bring his new wife back to England; there was no other way to keep her safe.

In early 1945 the pair married in Cracow, returning to England to make their home in Sheffield. During their journey home they came to know one another better and fell in love. The transition back into post-war Britain was hard for a German girl. Many families had lost young men fighting the war and the resentment towards Germany was intense. Ursula and Donald overcame the hate and prejudice and spent many happily married years together. Their story was picked up by the media – making front-page news – and was made into a play performed at Sheffield Royal Theatre and, in 1947, became a film, *Frieda*.

At dawn on 24 June Frederick Oliver's body was taken down from a willow tree adjacent to the crash site. One can theorise about just how he had been thrown clear of the wreckage, the most feasible explanation being it occurred on impact. Nearby, LM138 was a crumpled mess, burning and smouldering like a slain dragon taking its final breath. Ammunition was still exploding, as if in one last defiant act against its enemy. Monsieur Roger Caillau laid Frederick and Wilfred to rest in coffins crafted by his own hands. He took them to be buried in the local churchyard. The heroic gunner and courageous pilot, who willingly gave their lives to save others, were honoured in a joint burial.

The French people presided at the ceremony and laid flowers on the graves. Wilfred Cooke did not know for certain that his mid-upper gunner had been killed in the attack; as pilot and captain of the aircraft his responsibility was for the safety of his crew. Many men of lesser character would have left the doomed bomber to preserve their own life. This selfless act stands as testimony to a man who spent too little time on this earth.

No. 622 Squadron,
Royal Air Force,
Mildenhall,
Suffolk.

24th June, 1944.

Dear Mrs Oliver,

You will have received my telegram stating that your Husband, 1006958 Sgt. Frederick Oliver, failed to return from an operational flight on the night of 23/24th June, 1944.

He was the Mid Upper Gunner of an aircraft engaged on an important bombing mission over enemy territory, and after take-off nothing further was heard. It is possible that the aircraft was forced down, and if this is the case there is some chance that he may be safe and a Prisoner of War. In this event it may be two to three months before any certain information is obtained through the International Red Cross, although it is quite possible you may be the first to hear by having a card from your Husband. If this should be the case, would you please notify me, as the Squadron run a Prisoner of War Fund, and each month send comforts, cigarettes etc., to our Prisoners of War.

Your Husband had been with the Squadron only a short while, but during this time had made many friends. He was admired by all who knew him, and will be very much missed by us all.

His personal effects have been safeguarded, and will be dealt with by the Committee of Adjustment Officer, R.A.F. Station, Mildenhall, who will be writing to you in the near future.

May I, on behalf of the whole Squadron, express my most sincere sympathy, and hope you will soon receive good news.

Yours sincerely,

P. Swales.

(I.C.K. SWALES, DFC. DFM.)
Wing Commander, Commanding
No. 622 Squadron.

Mrs. K. Oliver,
1, Maple Grove,
Beech Hill, Wigan,
Lancs.

Left and following page Two official letters received by Kathleen. Wing Commander Swales informed Kathleen that her husband was missing in action. Overleaf is a letter from the Air Ministry relaying information from the German authorities about the crash. *Courtesy of K. Oliver*

Kathleen Oliver passed away on 28 July 2012, leaving behind for posterity her feelings and emotions within a number of poems. They are poignant and a wonderful illustration of dealing with personal loss.

The following is Kathleen's account of receiving the news of her husband's death:

I was cleaning windows upstairs at Maple Grove, Beech Hill. Everyone else was out when I noticed a young telegram boy on his bicycle, ride around Hazel Avenue. As I came downstairs our door knocker sounded. He looked at me anxiously as I opened the door. I opened the yellow envelope he handed to me. It was a rather large sheet. I read 'Do not communicate with the press. …'

I thought my husband (Sergeant Fred Oliver) had done something outstanding, and smiled at the boy and said, 'It's alright love'. The telegram was printed on both sides.

TELEPHONE :
GERRARD 9234
Extn. 3800

Any communications on the
subject of this letter should
be addressed to :—
THE
UNDER SECRETARY
OF STATE,
and the following number
quoted :— P.419191/5/44/P4.Cas.B4.

Your Ref. ....

AIR MINISTRY

(Casualty Branch),

73-77, OXFORD STREET,

W.1.

3rd August 1944.

Madam,

I am directed to refer to this Department's letter
dated 30th June 1944 notifying you that your husband, Sergeant
F. Oliver, Royal Air Force, was reported missing as the result
of air operations on the night of 23rd/24th June and to inform
you, with deep regret, that a telegram has been received from
the International Red Cross Committee, quoting German information, stating that Flying Officer A.W.Simmonds, Flight Sergeant
R.J.Hansford, Sergeant D. Meese, Flight Sergeant R.J.Chapman, and
Flight Sergeant T. Durrant were captured on the 24th June 1944,
and two members, whose identity the German Authorities are unable
to establish at present, belonging to the crew of this Lancaster
aircraft, lost their lives on that date.

As the crew consisted of seven members it would unhappily
appear that your husband is one of the two unidentified members
referred to as having lost their lives. I am to state, however,
that he will remain recorded as missing until confirmation of
the above telegram and burial particulars are received, or until,
in the absence of such confirmation, it becomes necessary owing
to lapse of time to presume, for official purposes, that death
has occurred. A further notification will be sent to you when this
action is taken.

In conveying the above information I am to extend to you
the Department's very deep sympathy in your grave anxiety.

I am, Madam,
Your obedient Servant,

for Director of Personal Services.

Mrs. F. Oliver,
1 Maple Grove,
Beech Hill,
Wigan,
Lancashire.

On the other side, which I read as he got on his bicycle – tentatively returning my smile – I read, 'We regret to inform you. …'

Telegram Boy

Lancs, England. 1944
Messenger from hell– unknowing.
Little boy with curly hair.
Streamers from your cycle flowing
As you pedal … where?
Yellow envelope in your pocket,
Bearing tidings dread; for whom?
Who will see this day of sunshine,
Blacker than the darkest tomb?
Who your face will long remember,
Stamped indelibly on my mind
As the last face they saw smiling
In the sun they left behind?
Telegram boy, please pedal slowly
Let them dream two minutes more
For their dreams will die for ever
When you knock upon their door
And he knocked upon my door
And smiled at me.

Kathleen Oliver 1947

The squadron's Operations Record Book (ORB) contains a succinct and unfeeling entry: 'Nothing further was heard from this crew after take-off.' History has pieced together the events of this tragic night; for those left behind the sense of loss and mourning would commence. Five of the crew would return home at the end of war to rebuild their lives and celebrate the freedom they helped to achieve. The families of Wilfred Harold Cooke and Frederick Oliver would

not be so lucky; both airmen became a loss statistic among the 55,573 airmen who lost their lives on active duty with Bomber Command. For them, the personal loss would continue far after the war and through the generations.

Today the small tranquil French graveyard continues to signify the fight against tyranny. Two airmen, one a New Zealander and one an Englishman, lie side by side in Socx churchyard. Their lives ended by a German night-fighter pilot whose intention was to defend his country. The Allied bomber was on an operation to protect and secure the freedom of those back home.

In September 2012, Kevin Oliver and his wife Virginia scattered his mother's ashes on his father's grave. Glancing across at the resting place next to his father's he respectfully read out the name on the tombstone, Monsieur Paul Vandaele, local farmer. All those years ago the wreckage of a fallen bomber had destroyed a section of his crop field. That event had made such an emotional impression on him that he wished to be buried next to the two airmen who gave their lives to liberate France. His wish was granted several years later. The bond between the aircrew is reciprocated by the civilians of the occupied countries they tried to liberate. The graves are tended and flowers are laid. There is no finer example of this bond than in the community of Socx.

The wedding vows made by Frederick and Kathleen in 1944 were not unusual: 'To love and cherish one another until death do us part.' Tragically death parted them prematurely; for one eternal peace, the other a lifetime of remembrance. Sixty-eight years later the circle of life was complete – it was only a matter of time. ●

Below left The two brave airmen buried side by side in Socx Cemetery France. *Courtesy of K. Oliver*

Below Kathleen Oliver touches a propeller from Lancaster LM138 during her visit to the crash site in 2006. A poignant moment in memory of her loss 62 years earlier. *Courtesy of K. Oliver*

CHAPTER TWO

'ABRACADABRA. JUMP!'

BY ROBERT OWEN

WHILE BOMBER COMMAND WAS DIVERTED TO ATTACK THE V1 LAUNCH RAMPS, THE ALLIED 'CROSSBOW' COMMITTEE WAS INCREASINGLY CONCERNED ABOUT LARGER CONSTRUCTIONS IN THE PAS DE CALAIS AT WATTEN, WIZERNES, MIMOYECQUES AND SIRACOURT. OF INDETERMINATE PURPOSE THEY WERE BELIEVED TO BE CONNECTED WITH THE IMPENDING ROCKET OFFENSIVE, BUT WERE IMPERVIOUS TO ORDINARY BOMBS THAT COULD AT BEST CHURN UP THE SURROUNDING AREA, TEMPORARILY DENYING ACCESS. TO DISABLE THEM PERMANENTLY WOULD REQUIRE MUCH A LARGER BOMB. ON 24 JUNE 1944 JOHN 'TEDDY' EDWARD AND HIS CREW WERE TASKED WITH DELIVERING JUST SUCH AN EXPLOSIVE.

THE REQUISITE WEAPON existed in the form of Barnes Wallis's 'Tallboy' deep-penetration bomb. Weighing 12,000lb with a strong steel case, this had been designed specifically for use against such hardened structures. While never intended to strike concrete directly, a 'Tallboy' dropped from high altitude and landing alongside such a structure would penetrate deep into the ground before detonation, causing a shock wave to travel through the earth in

located at Wizernes, 3 miles south of St Omer. Here tunnels had been driven into the face of a chalk quarry linking large excavated chambers that were intended for the assembly of V2 rockets, that would be taken out and fired from the floor of the quarry. The area above the underground assembly chambers was protected by a substantial concrete dome 300 feet in diameter and weighing 55,000 tons.

The squadron launched two daylight attacks against this site on 20 and 22 June, but both were

Left Preparing for dinghy drill: John Edward and crew, No. 50 Squadron, Skellingthorpe. L-R P/O Edward, Sgt McCulloch, P/O Pritchard, Sgt Brook, Sgt Casaubon, Sgt Isherwood, Front: Sgt Hobbs with the dinghy radio. *(All photos from the author's collection).*

the form of a minor earthquake in order to damage the structure's foundations.

'Tallboy' was initially allotted to only one squadron – No. 617 – who since their attack on the Ruhr dams in May 1943 had pioneered precision attacks against small targets using the Stabilised Automatic Bomb Sight (SABS). The squadron had first used the weapon against the Saumur railway tunnel on the night of 8/9 June, and after two further attacks against E-boat shelters at Le Havre and Boulogne their efforts were directed against the large V-sites. After an initial assault on Watten their attention switched to the site

aborted due to weather conditions over the target. Shortly before midday on 24 June orders were issued detailing sixteen Lancasters for another attempt that afternoon. The crews were again briefed and the aircraft prepared. Among the crews on the battle order was that of Flight Lieutenant John Edward, DFC.

Known familiarly as 'Teddy', 29-year-old Edward, from Bowden, Cheshire, had started the war as a gunner in the Royal Artillery but had been seconded to the RAF in 1941. After initial flying training he was commissioned with the temporary rank of pilot

Right A Tallboy shortly after release. The tail fins were offset 5 degrees to impart a stabilising spin. It would hit the ground travelling at the speed of sound.

officer in April 1943 and posted to No. 14 OTU at Cottesmore, where he assembled the genesis of his crew: Gerry Hobbs, a wireless operator from Reading and Sam Isherwood, aged twenty-two, an air gunner from Stretford, Manchester. The latter recruited another Lancastrian, from Southport, as bomb aimer: John Brook, twenty-one, a former Post Office engineer, had enlisted in 1941, having been inspired by the RAF's exploits in the Battle of Britain. Canadian navigator, Lorne Pritchard from Moose Jaw, Saskatchewan, completed the initial team. Transferring to No. 1660 Conversion Unit at Swinderby, the crew then added Irishman Bobby McCullough from Belfast as flight engineer and French Canadian Joseph Casaubon (known as 'Red' because of the colour of his hair), aged twenty-one, from Quebec, who joined as their second gunner. With the exception of Edward and Pritchard they were a non-commissioned crew. Having completed their conversion to the Lancaster the airmen were posted to No. 50 Squadron at Skellingthorpe on 28 June 1943.

For their first month at their new location, several of the crew found themselves used as fillers for other crews. McCulloch and Isherwood carried out an operation with Flying Officer Bolton against Essen in July. After a Lancaster flown by Sergeant Clarke crashed on take-off on 29 July one of his gunners, Sergeant Ron Pooley, a former van driver from Twickenham, opted to switch to Edward's crew, taking the place of 'Red' Casaubon. While these trips provided some members with operational experience it meant that the full crew did not commence operations in earnest until August, at the tail end of the Battle of Hamburg. The crew's entire tour was spent carrying out deep-penetration attacks against German city targets including Mannheim, Munich and Berlin, together with two operations against Milan during August in support of the Allied invasion of Sicily.

This was the period of German night-fighter ascendancy and fighters were seen on several occasions, requiring additional vigilance. Although their aircraft was equipped with the tail warning radar,

'Monica', it was unreliable and became unserviceable four times during their tour. Returning from Berlin on 18/19 November their disquiet on losing this equipment was compounded when they strayed over Lille and heavy flak started up, punching holes in the starboard side of the fuselage.

Ron Pooley opened fire on enemy aircraft during at least seven operations. On 23/24 August, while making the bombing run over Berlin, they were attacked by both a Ju 88 and Fw 190. Ron Pooley succeeded in dispatching the former, seeing it go down in flames, while Edward's extensive use of the cork-screw manoeuvre caused the Fw 190 to abandon its attack and seek easier prey. A month later, on 28 September, a further Ju 88 was destroyed on a sortie to Hanover. This was an eventful operation during which the crew had also to cope with the loss of W/T communication and the failure of Gee, selecting to land at Binbrook, the nearest base, rather than trying to locate Skellingthorpe.

Only on one occasion did the crew have to abort an operation. Setting out for Berlin on 23 December, failure of the rear turret heating resulted in Sam Isherwood contracting frostbite, necessitating an early return after jettisoning their bomb load in the North Sea.

By mid-December 1943 the crew were one of the most senior in No. 50 Squadron. Their persistence and determination were being recognised with the recommendation of awards, promulgated in February 1944. Edward and Pritchard received the DFC. The citation for the pilot remarked that he 'presses home his attacks regardless of enemy opposition. Both in the air and on the ground his courage and devotion to duty have been highly praised', while the navigator's 'skilful and very accurate navigation have been the key note of all his operational sorties' and 'his manipulation of special navigational equipment is of a high order and an example to the other navigators on his squadron.' The recommendation for Pooley's DFM recorded his successful combats and noted that 'his thorough search from his turret has prevented his aircraft from surprise attacks and on most occasions he has opened the combat with the enemy. This determination to engage the enemy at every opportunity is a fine example to the air gunners on the squadron.' By doing so Pooley was demonstrating the fighting spirit advocated by Air Vice Marshal Sir Ralph Cochrane, AOC No. 5 Group, whose policy of 'shooting first' to show enemy fighters that the bomber was no unsuspecting target was often at variance with many pilots who believed that it was best to hold fire until it was confirmed that the bomber had been seen.

In the eyes of higher authority these qualities had earmarked the crew for selection for either the Pathfinders or No. 617 Squadron. After considerable discussion the crew opted for the latter. On return from their twenty-fifth operation on 16 February 1944 – their eighth visit to Berlin – the crew transferred to Woodhall Spa where No. 617 Squadron, under the command of Wing Commander Leonard Cheshire, was still striving to regain full strength following their disastrous losses against the Dortmund–Ems Canal in September 1943. The squadron was engaged in attacks against factory targets in occupied territories, dropping the 12,000-lb HC blast bomb (not to be

Left Wizernes prior to attack. The quarry can be seen bottom centre and the concrete dome protecting the underground galleries, bottom right.

Right Wizernes under attack, 24 June 1944. F/O Don Cheney's bombing photograph taken from Lancaster KC-V.

confused with Wallis's later 12,000-lb 'Tallboy'). The first month was taken up by the crew practising the demanding teamwork required to achieve the required precision using the SABS. Illness, too, played a part in delaying their start on operations. For their first two sorties with the squadron, against Woippy on 15 March and the following night against the Michelin works at Clermont Ferrand, they carried Sergeant David Stewart as flight engineer, with Squadron Leader Don Richardson, the squadron's SABS instructor as bomb aimer for the latter operation.

The usual crew were together again for a successful attack against an explosives plant at Angoulême on 20 March. There then followed three less positive strikes against a factory at Lyons. A convincing assault against an aircraft repair plant at Toulouse marked the crew's thirtieth trip and official recognition of the completion of their first tour. Having just transferred to No. 617 Squadron, the expectation was that they would all opt to continue, without the usual rest period instructing at a training unit. However, Bobby McCullough and Ron Pooley saw things differently. Feeling that they had challenged the fates for long enough, both requested a rest, resulting in their posting the following month to No. 1660 CU, Swinderby, and No. 17 OTU, Silverstone, respectively. They would be replaced by Pilot Officer Leslie William John King as flight engineer and Flying Officer James Ian Johnston as mid-upper gunner.

Bill King had joined No. 617 Squadron at the age of thirty. He had completed his first tour of operations

Left and following page Wizernes showing the effects of intensive attacks. The area around the workings has been turned into a lunar landscape. The larger Tallboy craters can be easily identified.

with No. 57 Squadron, flying with New Zealander Pilot Officer Peter Singer, one of a pair of twins serving with the Squadron at that time. He participated in the low-level daylight attack against Le Creusot in October 1942; during this sortie the aircraft suffered a bird strike, one of them smashing the windscreen and injuring King about the face and eyes, which stopped him flying for four months. For his considerable fortitude and refusal to allow his injuries to distract other crew members, King had been awarded the DFC. In April 1943, while returning from Stettin, his aircraft was badly shot up over Denmark. The rest of the crew completed their tour in May but having only completed eighteen operations Bill transferred to the crew of Squadron Leader Ronald Smith for the remainder of his tour. In June he was injured in the

right foot during a raid on Wuppertal, resulting in a mention in dispatches. In August, while operating against Milan his aircraft was attacked over the Alps by a Bf 109, which the gunners claimed as a probable. After taking part in the Peenemünde raid, two further operations completed his tour. On joining 617 in November 1943 via No. 1668 Conversion Unit at Balderton, Bill was originally crewed with Wing Commander Cheshire, but became surplus at the beginning of April 1944 when Cheshire switched to a Mosquito to develop his new marking technique and Bill was thus available to join another crew.

King flew his first operation with Flight Lieutenant Edward's crew on 24 April. That night, while the main squadron marked Munich for a No. 5 Group attack, the airmen, with Flight Sergeant Frank Bell as rear

gunner, led six of the squadron's Lancasters to carry out a diversionary attack on Milan, in the hope of diverting night fighters further south. Returning from leave at the beginning of May the crew found themselves undertaking extensive navigation training in preparation for the D-Day deception, Operation 'Taxable'. For this Edward and his men doubled up with Australian Pilot Officer Ian Ross's crew to fly advancing orbits across the Channel, dispatching bundles of 'Window' to simulate an invasion convoy heading for the French coast north of Le Havre. Three nights later the airmen were among those of the squadron to introduce 'Tallboy' into service, with an attack against the Saumur railway tunnel.

Ian Johnston joined No. 617 Squadron from No. 619 Squadron on 1 May as a 'spare' gunner. Aged twenty-six, he was a tall six-footer from Ontario. He had left school in 1935 and worked originally as a shedman for the Temiskaming and Northern Ontario Railway before becoming a diamond driller at the Kerr Addison goldmine in Virginiatown. He applied for military service in June 1940 and attended a basic training camp at North Bay, Ontario, during the last months of the year to qualify for the military reserve. With a brother already a wireless operator in the RCAF he looked to the same service, seeking to become either an equipment assistant, or pilot/observer. He was deemed suitable for aircrew and in September 1941 was enrolled for training. The start of 1942 saw him at No. 6 Initial Training School, and after two months

of poor results in mathematics and navigation he realised that he was never going to make the grade as a pilot or observer. At his own request he remustered as an air gunner and after a period of leave – during which he was married – he was posted to No. 6 Bombing and Gunnery School at Mount View, Ontario. Passing the course in sixteenth place out of thirty students, he was awarded his air gunner's badge on 17 July 1942. Rated as being of average performance he was promoted to sergeant, being recorded as 'reliable and hard working. He should make a good NCO.' The following month he arrived in the UK and was posted to No. 14 OTU at Cottesmore. Here, despite a bout of tonsillitis, his knowledge of both the theory and practice of gunnery improved, and he passed out with a 'good average', although was still not recommended for a commission. On posting to No. 1660 Conversion Unit at the beginning of March 1943 he teamed up with Acting Flight Lieutenant Ronnie Churcher and transferred with him to Woodhall Spa when Churcher was promoted to Squadron Leader to command A Flight of the recently formed No. 619 Squadron on 22 April.

Johnston missed Churcher's first two operations with the new squadron, and flew his first sortie against Krefeld on 21 June. Coincident with Edward's airmen, Churcher and his crew took part in Bomber Command's major attacks of this period, including that against Peenemünde, two against Hamburg (on one of which the DR (dead reckoning) compass became unserviceable while the aircraft faced a thunderstorm over the target), six against Berlin, and two against Milan. Flak caused a few small holes to their aircraft over Düsseldorf on 3 November, but their greatest challenge came during an attack on Berlin on 1 January 1944. By now the German night-fighter defences were becoming increasingly active, with fighters being directed into the stream en route to the target. Despite this, and with both their Monica warning radar and Johnston's turret becoming unserviceable, Churcher completed a successful attack. Churcher's second tour of twenty operations was achieved by the conclusion of January. Johnston, who had been commissioned at the end of December, required thirty in total to complete his first tour and transferred to Flight Lieutenant Norman Morrison's crew.

This was to prove a more eventful period. A month after his previous troubles over Berlin, Johnston's

Lancaster suffered an engine and electrical failure outbound to the German capital, necessitating abandonment of the sortie and the jettisoning of the bomb load and ammunition. Not long after, while attacking Stuttgart, the same engine caught fire and the following month, during an operation to Tours in a different aircraft, the crew experienced yet another engine fire. The following night, and no doubt to his relief, Johnston completed what was to be the final sortie of his tour. However, opting to continue on operations, he arrived on No. 617 Squadron to join Edward's crew as they began practice for 'Taxable'.

A switch to daylight operations occurred after the attack on Saumur as strikes against French targets brought about the need for additional accuracy. Despite Allied air superiority, dispensing with the cloak of darkness increased the potential risk of fighter attack, with the result that aircraft began to carry an additional crew member as an extra gunner. The squadron's first such attack was at dusk against E-boat pens at Le Havre, where the crew took Sergeant Stanley 'Chick' Henderson with them. Henderson would fly with them for two further operations, against Boulogne on 15 June and Watten on the 16th.

On 20 June they reverted back to a seven-man crew for an abortive operation against Wizernes, recalled owing to adverse weather over the target. For the operation against Wizernes on 24 June they would have a new additional gunner, nineteen-year-old Warrant Officer Tom Price.

Although Price was another Canadian, from Moncton, New Brunswick, Lancastrian roots were still evident. His father was a Canadian who had met and married a girl from Bury during the First World War and taken her back to Canada. Described as a 'very good type', he had been a clerk before joining up in October 1942. After training at No. 3 Bombing and Gunnery School, Macdonald, Manitoba, he travelled to New York to embark on a troopship for the UK, arriving on 11 May 1943. He undertook his first night flying at No. 29 OTU from Bruntingthorpe and its satellite Bitteswell, his gunnery being recorded as 'average'. Although assessed as future officer material, at the conclusion of the course he was posted as a sergeant to No. 1660 CU at Swinderby where he teamed up as rear gunner with Australian Pilot Officer Bill Carey and his crew. After transit through No. 5 Lancaster Finishing School the airmen were posted to No. 106 Squadron at Metheringham on 3 February 1944. They had completed only ten operations (including the Nuremberg raid of 30/31 March when No. 106 Squadron lost three out of seventeen aircraft) before being transferred over to No. 617 Squadron at Woodhall Spa as one of six crews posted in from various squadrons to provide an H2S capability for 617 in order to refine its marking technique. By 24 June Tom Price had flown eight operations with Carey and two further operations as an extra gunner with Australian Flying Officer Arthur Kell, against Le Havre and Boulogne on 14 and 15 June. He may also have flown as an additional gunner on the attack against Watten on 19 June.

Above The interior of the escape hatch of DV403 showing the quick release ring and spring loaded locking pin, with the leather strap handles to pull the hatch into the aircraft.

Left One of the rudder balance weights from DV403.

Right German diagram of the Tallboy.

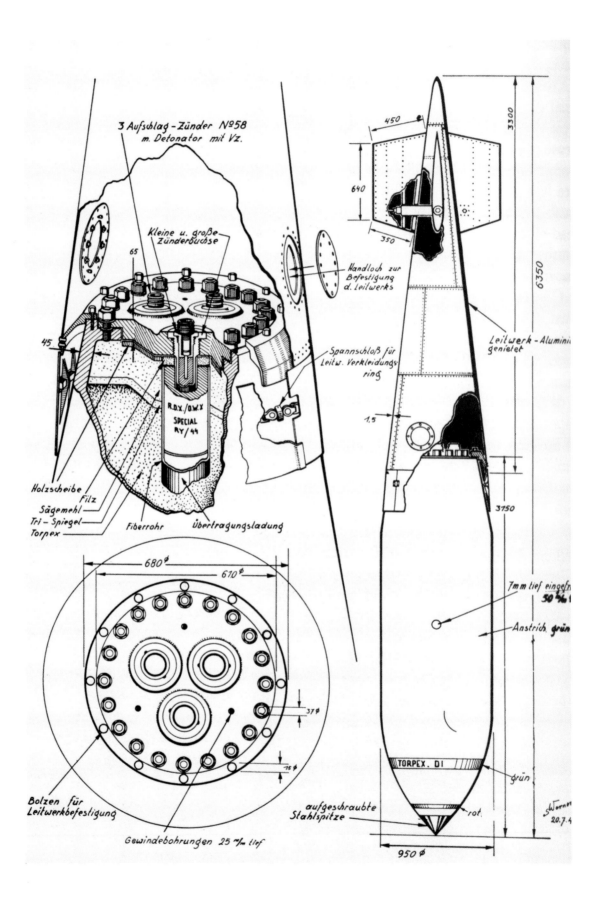

Left Wizernes dome
and quarry in 1984.

After briefing on 24 June, Edward and his seven colleagues took their pre-flight meal and gathered their flying clothing and other paraphernalia. There was a slight unease as the crew were driven out to dispersal. A heavy landing on the return from the abortive operation to Wizernes on 22 June had rendered the crew's usual Lancaster unserviceable; for this operation they were allocated a replacement aircraft, DV403, G-George. The concern soon passed as the crew boarded and became occupied with the task in hand. At 16.25 hours G-George lifted from Woodhall's runway. As the remainder of the squadron became airborne they formed into a loose gaggle and set course directly for North Foreland where, in a cloudless sky, they rendezvoused with an escort of Spitfires from No. 11 Group and headed for France. It was a warm summer's evening and to mitigate the greenhouse effect of Perspex and metal, many of the aircrew were flying in shirt sleeves, or battledress with their flying boots unzipped. The route from the Kent coast took them west of St Omer, from where they would commence their bombing run. Given the general Allied air superiority, Spitfire escort and additional air gunners, the threat from fighter attack was considered minimal. Of greater worry was the long, steady bombing run that was mandatory for SABS and essential if the squadron were to place their 'Tallboys' with the required precision. This was hazardous enough by night, but by day the aircraft would be an easily predicted target for any flak defences.

The attack opened at 17.50 hours. Wing Commander Cheshire attempted to mark the target in a Mosquito but his markers hung up. Flight Lieutenant Gerry Fawke then placed four smoke markers to indicate the general position of the target, leaving it to individual bomb aimers to identify their precise aiming point. Led in by Squadron Leader Les Munro, who was the first to bomb, and staggered at heights from 16,300 to 17,500 feet, the Lancasters commenced their assault, approaching the target from the northwest. Edward's aircraft was positioned about a third of the way back in the gaggle, flying at about 17,300 feet. As they approached the French villages of Moringhem and Zudausques, flak appeared ahead of the formation, with a tendency towards the higher aircraft. Suddenly two bursts hit Edward's aircraft. The first damaged the port wing, setting fire to both port engines. The second appeared to erupt beneath the aircraft, and red hot shrapnel perforated the rear fuselage, rupturing hydraulic lines and starting a further fire. It was obvious that the aircraft was seriously damaged. The first burst had seriously wounded, if not killed, Les King, the flight engineer; looking back Jack Brook could see him lifeless on the cockpit floor. Lorne Pritchard moved forward to attend to King, but found him beyond aid, having been hit in the head. John Edward made an instant decision and gave the order to abandon aircraft, 'Abracadabra, Abracadabra. Jump. Jump!'

Gerry Hobbs moved from his wireless operator's position and went aft over the main spar, intending to check on the rest of the crew and then bale out through the rear door. As he clipped on his parachute pack the 'chute began to deploy, the pack possibly having been damaged by shrapnel. Hobbs placed his arm across it to prevent the whole canopy spilling out. As he moved aft, at the rest bed he met Ian Johnston, who indicated that the fire at the rear was too intense to exit that way. The two men turned to go forward. As they reached the main spar, Hobbs could see activity in the cockpit. Brook and Pritchard had already left the aircraft via the nose hatch and John Edward was leaving his seat to follow them. Suddenly the aircraft began to shudder violently as it began its uncontrolled descent.

Witnesses on the ground watched the blazing aircraft fall. André Schamp, secretary of the local mairie and husband of the village schoolmistress, was gardening as the attack began. Seeing the burning Lancaster descending he ran in the direction of its likely impact. After passing over the village of Leulinghem and at a height of about 500 feet the aircraft exploded. The tail and port wing broke away, while the main wreckage landed in a field half a mile away. Looking up again, Schamp saw several parachutes descending, some not fully deployed. Reaching the crash site, and despite exploding ammunition, he located the remains of the cockpit in the burning wreckage, with the pilot, John Edward, lying face down. The body of Sam Isherwood lay nearby. Finding Johnston alive, but unconscious and badly injured, Schamp ran home to fetch a first-aid kit after removing Johnston's revolver from its holster. By the time he returned, German soldiers were at the scene. Schamp remained at the site until dusk, by which time, a further casualty, Tom Price, had been discovered, still in the remnants of his turret.

Hobbs recalled no more until he found himself lying in a field of oats, covered in cuts and grazes, his nose, right arm and right leg broken. He was surrounded by French civilians and German soldiers. Someone took a cigarette from his battledress pocket and lit it for him. Schamp gave him rudimentary first

aid as he was placed on lorry on a bed of straw alongside the badly injured Johnston, who was wrapped in his parachute and to whom Schamp had administered ether. They were taken to the hospital in St Omer to be treated, but Johnston's head injuries proved fatal and he died shortly afterwards without gaining consciousness. The Germans interred his body in St Omer's Longuenesse Cemetery.

The next day, a German Army lorry brought the bodies of Edward and Isherwood to Leulinghem where they were taken into the church and laid on cloths spread on the floor. Knowing that Price had been found, Schamp entered into negotiations with the Germans to have his body released for burial alongside his comrades, while work was started on three oak coffins and the sexton began to dig their graves. The three airmen were buried the following day after a short Roman Catholic service in the presence of a large number of villagers.

With three dead, three wounded, and one uninjured, the Germans believed that they had accounted for all of the Lancaster's crew. It was only a month later, when the horses drawing a local farmer's harvester stopped and refused to move forward, that the body of Bill King was discovered among the corn in field adjacent to the crash site where he had fallen, blown out of the aircraft when it exploded. The Germans refused permission to inter him at Leulinghem and took him to St Omer's Longuenesse Cemetery, where he was buried a short distance from Ian Johnston.

Jack Brook had jettisoned the nose hatch and was first to leave the aircraft, followed by Pritchard. As he descended beneath his parachute Brook saw several German soldiers raise their rifles towards him. He landed in a poppy field minus his boots that had come off as he left the aircraft, and was quickly apprehended by a group of soldiers who then marched him, in his socks, to the local village, where he was held until a car came to take him to St Omer. There the Germans attended to a small shrapnel wound in his buttock before interrogation. Pritchard, too, was captured and taken to St Omer and held in the same building as Brook. The following morning the two were transferred by lorry to the hospital where two stretchers, one carrying a heavily bandaged Hobbs, were loaded. They were moved to Lille, after which the three were split up again to be processed through Dulag Luft at

Oberursel. Arriving at the latter on 30 June, Brook experienced thirteen days' solitary confinement, during which he was subjected to alternate threats and moderate displays of charity. He was known to be a member of No. 617 Squadron and it is possible that the Germans were keen to learn more about 'Tallboy'. If so, they gained nothing from him. On 14 July he was sent to a transit camp at Wetzlar and after three days taken to a recently opened camp for RAF POWs, Stalag Luft 7 at Bankau (Bąków), 60 miles east of Breslau (Wrocław). Brook remained there until January 1945 when the prisoners were forced to travel on foot and in rail cattle trucks arriving at Stalag Luft IIIA, Luckenwalde, 32 miles south of Berlin, on 8 February. Although this camp was 'liberated' by Soviet troops

in the company of other injured Allied aircrew. After interrogation, which also tried to extract further information specifically about No. 617 Squadron, he was transferred to a POW hospital at Stalag IXC, Obermaßfeld, south-west of Erfurt. There he remained, with periodic moves to a nearby convalescent facility at Meiningen, until liberated by Patton's 3rd Army on 3 April 1945. Repatriated to the UK by Dakota he was initially received at the RAF hospital at Wroughton, before being transferred to Cosford.

For the next of kin there had been the dreaded telegram, followed by the confirmatory letter from the squadron commander. The latter usually propounded the possibility of the crew having survived and

Left The graves of John Edward, Sam Isherwood and Tom Price in Leulinghem churchyard were initially marked by simple wooden crosses.

on 22 April, the Russians refused to release the prisoners to an advance American party and Brook and a companion were forced to 'escape' through the wire on 6 May in an effort to contact US troops. This they did and Brook was taken to Brussels for repatriation to the UK by air and processing by Cosford. Lorne Pritchard was processed in similar fashion through Dulag Luft and sent to Stalag Luft I at Barth Vogelsang, where he would remain until set free in May 1945.

After further medical treatment in Lille, Gerry Hobbs experienced an eventful journey to Dulag Luft

evaded or been taken prisoner, but Cheshire's letter was forthright and honest, stating that the aircraft had been seen to be hit by flak while making its bombing run: 'After keeping a steady course for a short period of time, [it] dived to the ground out of control. Returning crews reported that two or three members of the crew were seen to bale out.' He continued: 'I feel it is my duty to tell you that I think that the rest of the crew, apart from these … would have little chance of survival, and all we can do now is wait for news from the International Red Cross.'

Right André Schamp, witness to the events that June afternoon, at the graves of John Edward, Sam Isherwood and Tom Price after the crosses had been replaced by the formal Commonwealth War Graves Commission markers.

Jack Brook's mother wrote to Wing Commander Cheshire saying that she had received notification from her son, dated 14 July, that he was safe and well. For the relatives of those who had died the uncertainty was prolonged. The RCAF Casualty Branch wrote to Ian Johnston's father announcing that his son was considered to be 'missing' – meaning that his whereabouts were unknown – but that for security reasons his son's name would not appear on casualty lists for five weeks. By 6 August information had been received, via the International Red Cross, that Flying Officer Johnston had been killed on 24 June. However, since this came from German sources he now would be listed as 'Missing – believed killed' until confirmed by other evidence or, failing that, after six months had elapsed with no further news. For Johnston's parents and widow, confirmation of death was only issued by the RCAF on 22 February 1945. But this only brought further uncertainty as to his place of burial. By 12 June examination of German records revealed that Johnston, Edward, King and another unknown airman had been buried in Longuenesse Cemetery, but the only grave number was that for King. Yet it was known that Edward had been interred in Leulinghem. Exhumation of this and adjacent graves

by an American team in August 1945 considered that the grave believed to contain Johnston actually held the remains of a US airman killed on 11 July. However, this body was subsequently identified in another grave. To add to the confusion the burial records kept by the Germans were found to be inaccurate after 1943, and it was later realised that this grave was in truth adjacent to that thought to contain Johnston's remains. As a result, a further examination was conducted by the RAF Missing Research and Enquiry Unit. Their report in December 1946 confirmed the remains wrongly attributed to those of a US airman were of an individual wearing only athletic shorts of a pattern favoured by Canadians. The fact that the body had no uniform was also indicative of a possible hospital death. The individual had suffered head injuries, and comparison of the teeth with dental records established that the remains were indeed those of Johnston.

However, it was only in August 1947 that confirmation was sent to Ian Johnston's father and widow, stating that his remains and grave had been formally identified. It would be a further three years until a permanent marker was erected and photographs of his final resting place were sent to his widow.

Postscript

The three survivors were known to be from No. 617 Squadron, and on reaching Dulag Luft, Oberursel, they were intensively cross-examined. Jack Brook's interrogator indicated a file on his desk, stating that a great deal was known about the squadron, but then went on to refer to Wing Commander Gibson as its commanding officer. This may have been a deliberate ploy to provoke a reaction and correction by the prisoner. If so, it did not work. Gerry Hobbs was likewise shown a map seemingly marking all No. 5 Group airfields, but with no reference to Woodhall Spa. In his case, after several days of questioning his captor entered the room announcing: 'Good morning, and how is Wing Commander Gibson and Wing Commander Cheshire this morning?', noting Hobbs's reaction. He then proceeded to talk of the skill of the Dams Raid, but that the defences had now been increased. The Germans wanted not only to learn more about the RAF's specialist squadron, but presumably were keen to acquire information about the squadron's new weapon, 'Tallboy'. The prisoners gave nothing away – but were not to know that the Germans were already obtaining 'Tallboy's' details from another source.

The Germans did their best to keep curious locals away from the wrecked Lancaster. The following day local farmer, André Rolin, who later discovered Bill King's body, made his way to the crash site on an agricultural pretext. While he was there several lorries arrived, carrying a large number of Russian prisoners of war, dressed in their striped overalls. Some started to remove sections of the wrecked aircraft and others began digging the earth.

After an hour or so they were seen to remove a large object, thought at the time by Rolin to be part of the aircraft. What he witnessed, however, was most likely the recovery of the first 'Tallboy' to be captured intact. It was manhandled on to a low trailer and taken away for dissection and examination. This assumption is reinforced by the fact that a detailed engineering drawing of 'Tallboy' appeared in a Luftwaffe technical manual describing Allied bombs, issued in December 1944.

The drawing, labelled 'Brit. Panzer-bombe SAP 12,000 lb, 5,400 Kg' was dated 20 July 1944 and can only have been created from inspection of a complete example, almost certainly from this aircraft. ◉

Left F/O Bill King's grave in St Omer Longuenesse cemetery.

Below
P/O Ian Johnston's headstone in St Omer Longuenesse cemetery.

CHAPTER THREE

NOT SO LUCKY

BY STEVE BOND

LIKE SO MANY OTHER MEMBERS OF BOMBER COMMAND, FLIGHT SERGEANT ROY OSWALD AND HIS CREW OF NO. 44 (RHODESIA) SQUADRON NEVER COMPLETED THEIR OPERATIONAL TOUR. HAVING ALL MIRACULOUSLY SURVIVED A LANDING ACCIDENT AT THE END OF THEIR FOURTH OPERATION, LESS THAN FOUR WEEKS LATER THEIR AIRCRAFT FELL VICTIM TO ONE OF THE LUFTWAFFE NACHTJAGD'S HIGHEST-SCORING NIGHT-FIGHTER ACES DURING AN ATTACK ON THE V1 LAUNCH SITE AT POMMERÉVAL. THIS TIME THEY WERE NOT SO LUCKY, WITH FOUR OF THE CREW LOSING THEIR LIVES, WHILE TWO WERE TO SUCCESSFULLY EVADE AND ONE WAS TO BECOME A PRISONER OF WAR.

OME OF THE crew had trained at Wellington-equipped No. 12 OTU at Chipping Warden in Oxfordshire, while others had been at No. 14 OTU, Market Harborough, in Leicestershire. Unusually, therefore, crewing up was not completed until they reached a Heavy Conversion Unit, following which the seven airmen were posted to No. 44 Squadron at Dunholme Lodge in Lincolnshire on 3 May 1944. Joining Southend-born pilot Roy Oswald were: flight engineer Sergeant Jim Hurley; navigator Flight Sergeant Archie Shoebottom, RCAF, from London, Ontario; air bomber Flight Sergeant Bill White from Aylesbury; wireless operator/air gunner Flight Sergeant Arthur 'Jake' Richardson from Epping; and air gunners Sergeants Les Hutchinson (also from Southend) and Bobby Sargent from Southampton.

Quickly thrown into the bombing campaign preparing for the D-Day invasion, Oswald first went on a familiarisation operation to an ammunition dump at Salbris in the Loire on the night of 7/8 May as second pilot to Flying Officer Joseph Bradburn, DFC, in Lancaster III ND517, KM-U; Roy's navigator, Archie Shoebottom, also went on the operation for experience, this time with Flying Officer Smith in ND869, KM-M. This proved to be very costly with seven Lancasters being lost including one from No. 44 Squadron, and ND517 came back with a damaged engine and a 24-foot-square hole in the port wing caused by the intense flak. Oswald's first trip as captain with the rest of his crew came two nights later in LL938, KM-S when their target was the engine works at Gennevilliers near Paris. Another squadron aircraft failed to return: ND515, KM-E, flown by Joseph Bradburn – who had taken Oswald on his first trip on the squadron – was brought down by the night fighter of Oberleutnent Heinrich Schulenburg of Nachtjagdgeschwader (NJG) 1./NJG4. Bradburn had only received his DFC on 24 April, and both his air gunners were holders of the DFM on their second tours; everyone on board the Lancaster perished.

Jake Richardson was then promoted to warrant officer and the airmen's next trip took place on the night of 11/12 May in LL938 to the Bourg-Leopold military camp in Belgium, passing without incident, although the bombing had to be halted as haze was causing aiming difficulties and there was a fear of hitting nearby housing. Oswald's crew then had quite a long wait until 27/28 May when they attacked the coastal battery at Morsalines in Normandy in brand-new Lancaster I ME794, KM-V, which had only arrived on the squadron three days previously. This time there was some confusion about the accuracy of the target marking, and they were told to stop bombing until the target location became clearer.

On the night of 31 May/1 June they took off at 23.09 hours for an operation against the coastal gun battery at Grandcamp-Maisy in Normandy, again flying ME794. However, due to heavy cloud over the objective they turned back and were diverted to land at No. 11 OTU's base at Westcott in Buckinghamshire just before 3 o'clock in the morning. Oswald attempted a late overshoot from his first approach to runway 07, which was high and fast. The aircraft careered off the end of the runway, crossing the main Aylesbury to Bicester road and was completely wrecked in a field beyond, bursting into flames. Fortunately, all the crew escaped injury and safely evacuated the plane. Just half an hour later, Westcott's duty flying control officer, Flight Lieutenant Edward Bulmer, went to inspect the scene just as the Lancaster's still intact 13,000lb bomb load exploded, killing him instantly. One of

Left
Sergeant Archie Shoebottom RCAF.
via Alain Trouplin

the engines was blown back across the road, causing major damage to a cottage that Flight Lieutenant Bulmer had just evacuated. The repairs to the roof can still be seen to this day. A witness to the accident, who was a twelve-year-old boy at the time, said that the fire got out of control because the emergency vehicles that had attempted to follow the path of the Lancaster had become caught up in the coiled barbed wire at the edge of the airfield. The crew of ME794 must have considered themselves extremely lucky to have escaped, and returned to Dunholme Lodge to continue their tour, with Archie Shoebottom celebrating his promotion to warrant officer.

They next flew on the early morning of 6 June in Lancaster I ME628, KM-V and thus took part in the D-Day assault with an attack on La Pernelle coastal gun battery. Their first bombing run had to be abandoned due to cloud obscuring the markers, but after a second orbit were sent in again and successfully dropped their bomb load. At 02.44 hours on 7 June they bombed Caen from 5,000 feet in the same Lancaster and despite a lot of smoke over the target, they felt the attack had been quite good. On the night of 8/9 June they took ME628 to Pontaubault in Lower Normandy for another successful assault, this time

on the railway being used by the Germans to bring up reinforcements.

This was followed the next night by a trip to Étampes airfield on the outskirts of Paris, in the same aircraft, and on this one occasion mid-upper gunner Les Hutchinson was replaced by Sergeant J.E. Beechey. Presumably Hutchinson was unwell, but the old crew were reunited again in time to take ME628 back to Caen on the 12th/13th.

The night of 16/17 June saw a change in target priorities, with a new focus on V1 storage and launch sites in the Pas de Calais. Oswald and his crew took their usual aircraft to the site at Beauvoir, the airmen reporting a 'straightforward trip with no trouble from defences'. In fact, no Bomber Command aircraft were lost that night despite a force of 405 flying against four separate sites. On 21/22 June the crew joined 132 other Lancasters attacking the very heavily defended synthetic oil plant at Wesseling in the Ruhr, which proved to be extremely costly – no fewer than thirty-seven aircraft were brought down when a large force of German night fighters managed to infiltrate the bomber stream. Of these losses, six were from No. 44 Squadron, a heavy toll indeed. ME628, however, was

Right The runway threshold at Westcott where Oswald's Lancaster overshot in the early hours of 1 June 1944.
Steve Bond

Left The Westcott house damaged by an engine from the exploding Lancaster. The dark area marks the repair. *Steve Bond*

lucky again and the crew reported little other than the fact that the target was totally obscured by cloud and that the bomb-doors open lights were not working.

They then found themselves detailed for what was to be their eleventh and last operation, this time against the V1 launch site at Pommeréval, north-west of Bellencombre in the Seine-Maritime region of northern France. On the night of 24/25 June, once again in ME628, they took off at 22.30 hours as part of a 739-aircraft force operating against various flying-bomb sites. The night was clear and moonlit, which not only facilitated bombing accuracy, but had the negative effect of making the job of the defending night fighters much easier. Aided by effective search-light cover, the NJG2, 3, 4 and 5 force slipped in among the bomber stream and ultimately accounted for four Lancasters attacking Pommeréval and a further eighteen from other targets. No. 44 Squadron's Operations Record Book describes the attack: 'Weather fine, slight haze, visibility 10–12 miles. 2–4 tenths cloud at 3,000 feet forming during the afternoon. 19 aircraft detailed to carry out a bombing attack on Pommereval. Flt Sergeant Oswald and Plt Off Aiken were reported missing without trace from this operation. All other

aircraft reached and bombed the target successfully and returned to base safely. Appeared to be a good concentrated attack and fires were seen in the target area. All pilots think this raid to have been successful.'

It would appear that a Lancaster claimed by Major Paul Semrau of Stab.II/NJG2 was in fact Aiken's ND751, KM-J. Doug Aiken was an RCAF officer and sadly his entire crew perished.

With the target bombed between 23.51 and 00.17 hours, Oswald's crew had completed their task and turned towards St Valery and home when, at 00.16 hours, it came under attack from a Ju 88, causing sufficient damage for the skipper quickly to realise that the aircraft was out of control and he ordered the crew to abandon it. Sources have suggested that the night-fighter pilot concerned was either Ober-leutnant Heinz Rökker of 2./NJG2 or Major Semrau, both having claimed a Lancaster at about the same time in roughly the same area, ME628 coming down close to the village of Bellencombre. Rökker's claim was timed at 00.16 hours, with a location just south of Dieppe at a height of 9,200 feet. With his crew comprising Bordfunker (radio/radar operator), Feldwebel Carlos Nugent, and Beobachter (observer), Unter-

Right No. 44
Squadron Lancaster
I R5729 KM-A at
Dunholme Lodge
prior to the 2 January
44 Berlin raid.
IWM CH11929

offizier Fritz Wefelmeier, he recorded the event as follows: 'We had moved to Châteaudun but there was no gasoline, and so we took gasoline from the other 'planes. On 25 June the RAF made attacks on the launching sites of the V1; I saw five or six at the same time and I could shoot them down as I was beneath them. There was no return fire, they did not see me. I shot a Lancaster with my crew in Ju 88 G-1 4R-CK south from Dieppe at 00.16 hours at a height of 2,800 metres [9,200 feet] with a burst of fire from the Schräge-Musik. I had taken off from Châteaudun at 23.25 and landed at 02.25 at Eindhoven.'

The second possible victor, Major Semrau, timed his claim at 00.17 hours, also south of Dieppe at a height of just 5,900 feet. He had probably already shot down No. 44 Squadron's ND751 a few minutes earlier, but it would seem that his second claim was most likely a follow-up attack on Oswald's descending aircraft, which was already doomed after Rökker's attack. This is borne out by the subsequent testimony of surviving crew members, who spoke of two separate attacks. It was Rökker's thirty-third victory, and he went on to finish the war with a final total of sixty-four.

With the Lancaster badly on fire from three or four cannon-shell hits to the starboard fuel tanks, only the forward section crew members Jim Hurley, Archie Shoebottom and Bill White were able to exit via the escape hatch. When Oswald gave the bale-out order, Shoebottom donned his parachute, by which time White had already jumped. Hurley seemed reluctant to go, but eventually did so, followed finally by Shoebottom. The latter's parachute took some time to open and he became aware of a fire on the ground, realising as he landed that it was the remains of the Lancaster, which had come down in woods on the outskirts of Bellencombre and been completely destroyed, the wreckage being scattered over an area of several hundred square yards.

Roy Oswald stayed at the controls for as long as possible to allow his crew to get out, by which time the aircraft was too low for his own attempt, and he perished in the crash along with crew members Arthur Richardson, Les Hutchinson and Bobby Sargent. Sadly, Oswald's body was never found and he is commemorated on Panel 221 at the Runnymede Memorial, but the other three were subsequently buried in a collective grave in Bellencombre Communal Cemetery.

Of the three survivors, Jim Hurley was initially able to make contact with the local Resistance but despite this he was eventually captured and became a prisoner of war in newly built Stalag Luft 7 at Bankau, 65 kilometres west of Breslau in Silesia, where he would see out the rest of the war. Archie Shoebottom and Bill White had rather better luck, as recounted in the evasion reports they completed on their return, both making it back to England on 9 September and being interviewed the next day. Archie recalled what happened as they came away from the target and were initially attacked by what he thought was an Fw 190, which apparently only made a single pass after being scared off by the Lancaster's air gunners. The subsequent successful attacks came unseen from under the aircraft using the Ju 88's notorious upward-firing Schräge-Musik cannons:

Soon after leaving the target we were shot down by a fighter, and I baled out at about 00.20 hours, landing near a wood by Orival. I hid my parachute etc., in this wood, but they were later collected and hidden or destroyed by a French person. I remained in the wood until 15.00 hours, when a man came along [Dr Valles].

and give up the idea of going to Spain. On 28 June this man [Dr Valles] drove me to a house in St. Saëns where I stayed until 2 July. I was then moved to another house in the same town where my bomb-aimer Flt Sergeant White was living. We both lived there until the Allied forces arrived on 31 August.

While hiding in the first location, Shoebottom was contacted by Madame Valles, who asked him about his crew, squadron and their target. She took a copy of his identity card and told him that Bill White had also landed safely and was in their hands. It further transpired that although Jim Hurley had made contact with the Resistance, he had subsequently been captured. Shoebottom also handed over the photograph of himself in civilian clothes that all aircrew carried in case of landing in occupied territory. A day or two later it was returned to him on a false identification card for an agricultural labourer by the name of Louis Duval.

The building close to Saint-Saëns where he was first taken was a windmill, the home of a Monsieur

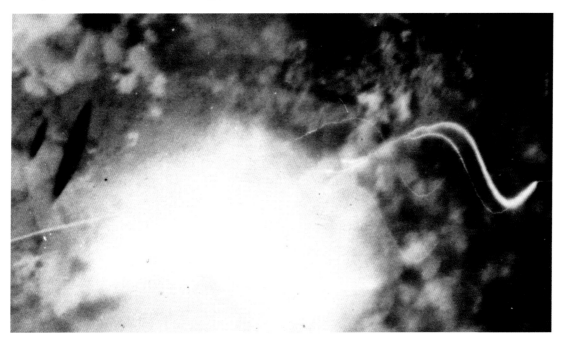

Left A Ju 88 over Pommeréval on 24/25 June 1944, taken from a No. 49 Squadron Lancaster. *Air 27 484B*

After I had watched him for half an hour I made myself known to him. I hid again and he went away, returning in the evening with food and a friend [Albert Prieux], who later took me to his house in Orival. He gave me civilian clothing, and I stayed there three days, during which time a man advised me to move to a safer place

Guedon and his wife, who both proved to be very friendly. Much to Shoebottom's delight, they provided a special meal on 1 July in honour of Canada's Dominion Day. The following day he was taken into the centre of Saint-Saëns, which was full of German troops, strolling around, gathering in groups and

Right Oblt Heinz Rökker. *Heinz Rökker*

busy chatting and laughing. Shoebottom and his escort managed to move among them undetected and made their way to the door of a café. Madame Valles knocked and they were admitted by a man known by the sobriquet 'Guardian Angel'. This was Michel Legardien, of the Resistance, who lived there with his wife Suzanne. Bill White was already present, having arrived a few days earlier.

White must have been the last man to leave the burning Lancaster, timing his escape from it at 00.30 hours, almost a quarter of an hour after it was first attacked:

I landed in the Forêt d'Eawy. I had to leave my para-chute in the trees. I left my Mae West, 1/6d [one shilling and six pence], and Form 3073 about 50 feet from where I landed in a northerly direction to mislead searchers. I started walking south but decided to hide in the bushes, and slept until dawn.

At 05.30 hours I started walking and eventually met a man to whom I declared myself as English, asking him where the nearest Germans were, as I wanted to surrender. He did not seem interested, but the next man I asked took a dim view of my wanting to surrender. Having made sure of my man, I asked where I could get help. He gave me a blank identity card and directed me to Bosc Beranger, where a helper gave me civilian clothes, food and ration cards for a month, and filled in my identity card. I stayed the night here and on 27 June he handed me over to a man at St. Saëns, where I stayed until 29 June. This café was full of Germans, and I was handed over to another man in the same town, with whom I stayed. I was in touch with the Resistance through several people, and they advised me to wait for the Allied forces, rather than attempt to get

Right Rökker's Ju 88 crew; L to R Carlos Nugent, Heinz Rökker, Franz Franz (ground crew), Hans Mattar, Fritz Wefelmeier. *Heinz Rökker*

Left Orival clearing on the edge of Forêt d'Eawy where Archie Shoebottom landed.
Alain Trouplin

away on my own. On 2 July I was joined by my navigator Warrant Officer Shoebottom and from this date my story is the same as his. We both left France on 9 September.

Having been reunited, Shoebottom and White were put up in a spacious room with large windows, overlooking a garden surrounded by a wall, offering them good security. Every day Mr Legardien went by bicycle to get food and was usually able to find meat, eggs and fresh vegetables for Madame Legardien to provide food, which Shoebottom described as being 'much better than in the mess in England!' Across the street from the café was the local German headquarters. Each morning large numbers marched out, carrying picks and shovels, and returning in the evening. It was thought that they were working on V1 launch ramps as the two airmen could sometimes hear one being fired, so they knew the site was close by; in fact it was almost certainly the very same site at Pommeréval that they had been bombing, showing that it had probably not suffered major damage. As the invading Allied forces came closer, it became extremely dangerous to move about by day due to attempts to bomb the site, and the two men made much use of the prohibited

BBC News in order to track the progress of the war.

It soon became obvious, judging by the aerial activity and the growing unrest among the Germans, that the arrival of Allied troops was imminent. Then on 31 August the remaining Germans packed up and left the building opposite, machine-gun fire could be heard coming from the outskirts of the town, and shortly afterwards patrols from the 2nd Canadian Division arrived, just as the last of the enemy disappeared in the opposite direction. A friend of Monsieur Legardien offered to take the two former evaders to Rouen, and with the help of the Allied forces they were able to finally get away, having bid a fond farewell to the Legardiens. A few days later Shoebottom and White were flown back to Northolt.

Neither man appears to have returned to No. 44 Squadron and their further service is unknown. A replacement crew would have taken over from them as soon as they were reported missing and, by that stage of the war, the number of new crews coming out of training was starting to exceed losses by quite a margin. After the war Archie Shoebottom moved to the United States and took out American citizenship. In 1974 he was reunited with the Legardiens in New York. ●

CHAPTER FOUR

'THE BOY I CHERISH AND LOVE WITH ALL MY HEART'

BY STEVE DARLOW

TWO OF THE MOST CRITICAL ATTACKS IN BOMBER COMMAND'S V1 COUNTER-OFFENSIVE TOOK PLACE ON THE NIGHTS OF 4/5 AND 7/8 JULY 1944. ALLIED INTELLIGENCE HAD LED TO THE IDENTIFICATION OF THE CAVES AT SAINT-LEU-D'ESSERENT AS A MAJOR FLYING BOMB SUPPLY DEPOT. RAF BOMBER COMMAND RESPONDED WITH TWO MAJOR NIGHT RAIDS. THE FIRST, INVOLVING 231 AVRO LANCASTERS AND 15 DE HAVILLAND MOSQUITOES, WAS DEEMED A PARTIAL SUCCESS, WITH THE LOSS OF 13 LANCASTERS AND CREWS. BOMBER COMMAND CREWS, MANNING 208 LANCASTERS AND 13 MOSQUITOES, RETURNED THREE NIGHTS LATER, COMPLETING A DEVASTATING ATTACK THAT SERIOUSLY DISRUPTED, AND SUBSTANTIALLY DIMINISHED, THE SCALE OF THE V1 OFFENSIVE. GERMAN NIGHT FIGHTERS, HOWEVER, HAD EXACTED THEIR TOLL, ACCOUNTING FOR MOST OF THE 29 LANCASTERS AND 2 MOSQUITOES THAT FAILED TO RETURN. AT THE CONTROLS OF ONE OF THOSE LANCASTERS WAS NO. 207 SQUADRON'S TREVOR HORDLEY.

TEN WEEKS EARLIER Trevor had married his long-time sweetheart Muriel Hillyard. They had met in a dance hall in Rugby and during their courtship Muriel had endured his long absences while Trevor trained as pilot with the Royal Air Force, which included almost a year overseas. They kept in touch by letter, of course, and she had treasured photographs, including one of a youthful and happy Trevor where she had written on the back: 'The boy I cherish and love with all my heart.' On 29 April 1944 the couple got married, with Trevor returning to his unit the following day. When the awful 'deeply regret to inform you …' telegram arrived in July 1944 Muriel, who already knew she was pregnant, collapsed.

Trevor Hordley was born on 15 April 1920 at Pembroke Dock, Pembrokeshire, the third son of Frederick and Sarah, enlisting with the Royal Air Force Volunteer Reserve (RAFVR) in August 1941. Prior to joining the RAF Trevor had moved from Pembroke Dock to Rugby where he worked as a 'turner' at the British Thomson-Houston engineering works. New RAFVR recruit Trevor arrived at No. 1 Aircrew Reception Centre on 16 February 1942, with subsequent postings to No. 8 Initial Training Wing and No. 26 Elementary Flying Training School. A trip across the Atlantic followed, Trevor reaching Canada on 6 September 1942, and arriving at the US Naval Air Station, Pensacola, Florida, on New Year's Day 1943.

An air letter, postmarked from Moncton, Canada, and dated 17 September 1942, was sent to his brother in England, Sergeant Neville Roy Hordley (116th Royal Welsh Light Anti-Aircraft Regiment). Trevor provides the details of his journey to 'Roy': 'I have arrived in Canada safely and I had a wonderful trip across. I also had a trip of 800 miles in the train across America and I saw some lovely country. I won't be in this place very long before proceeding to Florida to do my training and the sooner I get weaving on the course the better.' Trevor commented on the ship he sailed in as 'a beauty' and the 'wonderful food ever since we left England … oranges, pears, grapefruit and as much chocolate as money can buy'. However, Trevor remained keen to progress, 'The weather is lovely and we are being issued with tropical kit in readiness for our trip down South. I don't think a lot of the place and the quicker we are out and on the

Left 'Taken on 28 February 1942, 'Lots of Love Trevor'. *All photos courtesy of the Hordley family.*

course the better it will please me.' Trevor closed the letter with a 'warning' to his brother: 'Well Roy I must close now, please keep in touch with Muriel and try to meet her sometime only don't get too friendly otherwise I will get nasty.'

On 10 April Leading Aircraftman Hordley wrote to his parents from 'British Flight Battalion, Box no. 212, U.S. Naval Air Station, Penascola':

Dear Mam & Dad
I received your letter and birthday card OK on April 6th, your letter was dated March 10th. …

Well I start flying Catalinas on Monday and so that will be quite a change after what I have been used to. … I will be going for long sea trips over the Bay of Mexico now and three students will go up at a time. While the other two are flying I will get into one of the bunks and catch some shut eye. I have just completed a week's gunnery and oh boy am I pleased. I came out top in revolver shooting by scoring 234 points out of a possible 245, the next highest score to mine was 188. I also shot 150 shells at clay pigeons but did not do so good as expected. …

Right now we are having an electric storm and the flashes are wizz and remind me of a good night's raid on Coventry. The heat too is getting terrific and after a good deal of moving around it is nothing to see some chaps soaked to the skin with perspiration, although I don't perspire to that extent. It takes me a long while to get to sleep at nights in this heat and also a long time to wake me up in the mornings. We now get up at 5.45 am instead of 5 am, which is to my approval. They have eliminated the morning P.T. but I smell something else cooking as I know they couldn't be so kind as this. …

again I will have to start all over because I've forgotten any technique I ever knew. This does not sound like America but it is actually what goes on around here, dances are strictly for American cadets only, and it is not the nice thing to say but it eats my heart out to think of the good times the Yanks were having in Manchester. …

Six months later and Trevor was back in the United Kingdom, destined to serve with RAF Bomber Command and passing through various training units including No. 14 Operational Training Unit on

Right The Hordley family. Front left to right, Frederick Hordley, Sarah Anne Hordley, Daniel Hordley. Back from left, Trevor Hordley and Roy Hordley.

A pal of mine, a Londoner and cockney, went to New Orleans last week and he went up to a British petty officer & asked him if he knew where he could get a good drink of beer. The petty officer replied, 'Gawd Blimey, I ain't had a decent drop of bloody wallop since I left the Old Country.' My pal said he sank to his knees laughing and caused quite a scene in doing so. …

A young lady spoke to me the other evening in the movies. She said 'pardon me' because she wanted to pass. I blushed at the thought of a female actually speaking and all the lads wanted to know what she said and called me a lucky devil. When I see Muriel

his way to No. 207 Squadron at RAF Spilsby, arriving there in May 1944. The previous month he had married Muriel, and could also celebrate having been 'granted a commission for the emergency as Pilot Officer (on probation)'.

Prior to the July raids on the caves at Saint-Leu-d'Esserent, Trevor and his crew had been extremely active in supporting the Normandy invasion and countering the V-weapon threat. On the night of 3/4 June Trevor's Lancaster had been one of ninety-six from No. 5 Group that had carried out a devastating attack on the German signals station at Ferme-d'Urville, following up the next night with a raid against the coastal gun battery at Maisy. On the eve of D-Day Trevor had piloted his crew in an assault on an enemy communications target at Caen. Throughout June Trevor's logbook filled with the basic details of his sorties, brief entries that often hid the drama of the operation; on the raid to Étampes rail-yards on 9/10 June the crew managed to survive two encounters with enemy aircraft, and witnessed another Lancaster blow up directly in front of them. Having had his logbook stamped and the month of June signed off, the entries for July began to accumulate, two of which recorded his involvement in one of the most effective interventions against Hitler's reprisal weapons. Sadly, the entry for the raid on the night of 7/8 July would not be completed by Trevor's hand.

Since the opening salvo three weeks previously, and with no let-up in the enemy's V1 offensive, Allied intelligence used all means available to try and identify the best targeting policy to diminish the scale of attack. Enigma decrypts had suggested that underground depots provided the link between the production of the V1s and the launch sites. Indeed, in March 1944 the Special Operations Executive had identified an underground flying-bomb store at a place called Saint-Leu-d'Esserent. On 29 June the Air Ministry sent a cypher message to the Allied Expeditionary Air Force, asking that the caves at Saint-Leu-d'Esserent be given priority status for a raid. An Enigma decrypt effectively reported a 'goods in, goods out' at Saint-Leu-d'Esserent. The caves were clearly a critical node within the V1 supply system. The heavy bombers of Bomber Command were called upon to intervene.

On 4 July 1944 Trevor Hordley's crew were detailed to attack the underground caves at Saint-Leu-d'Esserent, Bomber Command dispatching a total of 231 Lancasters and 15 Mosquitoes in an attempt to smash the V1 supply depot. Taking off in ND567 the crew delivered their eleven 1,000-lb and four 500-lb bombs despite being fired on by a Lancaster while orbiting the target. German night fighters proved the main threat that night, accounting for most of the thirteen Lancasters lost, including two from No. 207 Squadron, with only one man surviving. In the following hours and days Allied intelligence sought to gather information in regard to the outcome of the raid. Initial assessment suggested some success, with

accurate marking and bombing in excellent weather conditions. Reconnaissance showed cratering in the target area and what appeared to be considerable damage with numerous craters, and it appeared that a section of the cave roof had collapsed. The Germans also seemed to be feverishly working on repairs. Notable, however, was the interception of a German signal sent just after the raid and summarising the effect of the attack: 'Installation attacked by heavy bombers. … Several hundred bombs of heavy and heaviest calibre dropped. Cavern entrance clear, approach roads, railway installations destroyed. App-

Left Taken while training and written on the back, 'The main stay of the RAF Hordley and Colley'.

roach from St Leu probably repaired within 24 hours. Casualties among ammunition depot personnel 5 men missing. Among flak personnel 5 dead, 6 wounded and 6 to 7 missing. In cavern no penetrations. Communications out of action.'

Clearly the extent of the damage was not what the Allies had hoped for. Bomber Command would need to visit the caves again.

Three nights after their first visit to Saint-Leu-d'Esserent, the Hordley crew were again detailed as one of sixteen No. 207 Squadron crews to be part of the 208 Lancaster and 13 Mosquito force sent back to the caves to hopefully finish the job. That night five of the squadron's aircraft would not be returning to RAF Spilsby, with half the men flying these Lancasters not surviving.

There was quite a complicated raid plan for the Bomber Command attacks that night. In addition to the Saint-Leu-d'Esserent bombing there was a 128-aircraft attack on the Vaires railyards, diversionary sweeps, radio countermeasure sorties, drops to the Resistance, and Mosquito raids on targets in Germany – 634 sorties in total. The force sent to Saint-Leu-d'Esserent was to form three waves on the outward leg of the flight, with the largest wave sharing their approach with the Bomber Command unit that was detailed to attack the railyards at Vaires. To the west of Paris the Vaires force would continue south, with the Saint-Leu-d'Esserent large wave turning and flying to a rendezvous with the other waves to the south-west of the caves. It was hoped the German night-fighter controllers would believe that the main assault that night was to be to the south of the French capital. The bombing of the V1 depot was scheduled to open at 01.10 hours with Mosquitoes finding and marking

Right Taken at Primrose Hill, Regents Park on 25 February 1942, Trevor Hordley is second from the left on the back row.

the aiming point a few minutes prior to the main bombing assault.

At RAF Spilsby, Trevor Hordley lifted his Lancaster from the runway at 22.45 hours, with navigator, William 'Mac' Brown, directing his skipper to their place in the bomber stream, flying across the English Channel and heading south-east from the French coast prior to reaching the three-wave rendezvous point just before 01.00 hours. It was around this time, as the bomber stream prepared to fly direct to the target, that the battle between Bomber Command and Luftwaffe night-fighter airmen began in earnest. With the attack opening on the V1 supply depot, many RAF crews now witnessed the demise of their colleagues in other aircraft as combat raged. Tracer tore through the darkness, engines burst into flames, and burning aircraft plummeted to the ground. Amid this aerial melee Trevor Hordley successfully reached the target and dropped his bombs. The stream split again as it left the target, into three waves, but the German night fighters gave chase. One RAF bomber came into the sights of one such night fighter – that

Right clockwise
Muriel's personal picture of Trevor with 'The boy I cherish and love with all my heart', written on the back; Trevor Hordley, seated in the middle at Club Bali, New Orleans; Taken at Penascola in March 1943 Trevor stands on the right.

flown by Trevor Hordley – and at 01.44 hours on the morning of 8 July 1944 Lancaster ND567 and its seven-man crew were shot from the night sky, the flaming bomber falling to earth on the edge of some woods near Sérifontaine, north of Gisors and to the west of Beauvais. Only two men survived the incident. Flight engineer George Baker, as shall be seen later, was extremely fortunate to get out of the stricken aircraft, parachuting to earth and managing to evade for a short time before capture, seeing out the war as a prisoner. Navigator William 'Mac' Brown was similarly fortunate and was hidden until Allied forces liberated the area a couple of months later. But 24-year-old Trevor Hordley lost his life, along with 23-year-old Canadian bomb aimer Hugh Burgess, 20-year-old wireless operator Fred Booth, and 19-year-old air gunners Alan Holmes and Gerald Cooper. All five now rest in Commonwealth war graves at the Marissel French National Cemetery, Beauvais. The attack on Saint-Leu-d'Esserent did prove successful

and seriously disrupted the German V1 supply system and diminished the flying-bomb assault upon London. But the price was high – the German night fighters accounted for most of the 29 Lancasters and 2 Mosquitoes that were lost that night. Over 200 'deeply regret to inform you' telegrams now had to be sent to the next of kin of those who perished, including the soon-to-be mother and newly-wed wife of Trevor Hordley.

Any hope that Trevor may have survived the ordeal was dashed when news reached his family later that year. On 23 November 1944, Trevor's father Frederick wrote to Mrs Burgess:

I am deeply grieved to inform you that we have received information from the Air Ministry that my son Pilot Officer Trevor John Hordley and 4 other members of his crew are dead and that one member Sergt. Baker is a prisoner of war in Germany and that another one whose name I do not know, is in England.

Left Trevor Hordley and Muriel May Hillyard on their wedding day 29 April 1944; Flying Officer Trevor John Hordley.

My daughter-in-law informs me that in a paper called 'Aeroplane' published in England, the names of 6 members of the crew are reported as 'Missing', but does not give the name of the 7th. The name not included in the list is that of the Navigator named Brown and therefore I am assuming this must be the one who is in England.

My son spent 12 months training in the United States of America at Grosse Ile near Detroit and at Pensacola in Florida. He always spoke very highly of his crew and felt very proud of them and I am sure from what he told me that they were a very happy crowd and had every confidence in each other and it is terrible to think that such fine young men should be sacrificed in horrible war.

We have two other sons in the Forces and as we ourselves have been bombed out of our home on two occasions we consider that we have had our share of trouble and grief.

My wife and I feel very very sorry for you all in

your distress and we know only too well what all this has meant to you. The anxiety when we heard over the Radio that the Lancasters had been out on the previous night was very trying and every visit of the Postman made one shudder.

I am extremely sorry that I cannot give you some hopeful information but I am afraid that my wife and I are now resigned to the fact that in view of what the Red Cross say, there is now no ground for hope.

On 11 December 1944 the Hordleys received a letter back from an S. Chas Burgess in Canada.

We, like you, are now prepared to see this thing in its hard reality, unfortunately. We send you our very, very deep sympathy; we know what a bottomless pit it means to anyone, but somehow we must strive to fill it up, or at least bridge it over. You have your share now apart from what has happened to you; I was

Oblique aerial photograph showing the entrances to the subterranean tunnels at St Leu D'Esserant, north-west of Paris, which were used by the Germans to store flying bombs. An accurate attack by Bomber Command aircraft on the night of 7/8 July 1944 succeeded in causing a landslide which blocked the tunnel entrances.

Air Historical Branch

Right A pair of photographs showing damage to the cave entrances to the V1 storage depot at St Leu D'Esserant, following the RAF Bomber Command raids of July 1944. *Air Historical Branch.*

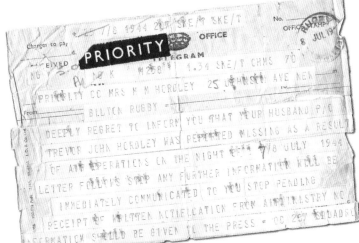

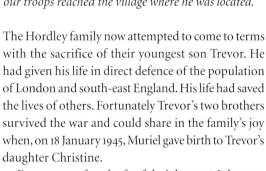

through the last one, so know something of what War means. We are able to give you a little information you have not yet received. We have heard from Brown, now P/O W. R. Mc. Brown, he tells us the 'plane was shot down, and as I see it, the Oxegen [sic] and petrol tanks were punctured, this may be wrong, but that is how I see it. He passed out and fell into the flames about his table when his Oxegen lead failed and came to in mid-air, pulled his rip-cord and landed although burned. The French people took care of him for two months, and he got back when our troops reached the village where he was located.

The Hordley family now attempted to come to terms with the sacrifice of their youngest son Trevor. He had given his life in direct defence of the population of London and south-east England. His life had saved the lives of others. Fortunately Trevor's two brothers survived the war and could share in the family's joy when, on 18 January 1945, Muriel gave birth to Trevor's daughter Christine.

Forty years after the fateful night, on 8 July 1995, the flight engineer George Baker accompanied Air Vice Marshal David Dick, President of the No. 207 Squadron RAF Association, to lay wreaths at the dedication of a stone memorial commemorating the crew of Lancaster ND567 – the bomber having crashed in the woods to the rear of the memorial. Then, in June 2013, brother and sister Peter Hordley and Pauline Cole, Trevor's niece and nephew, visited the memorial, (Christine was unable to attend owing to ill health) accepting the presentation of a piece of the Lancaster wreckage and placing wreaths at the foot of the commemorative stone etched with the words 'Morts pour la Liberté souvenez vous'. ●

Left, from top
'Deeply regret to inform you …' telegram; Peter Hordley and his sister Pauline Cole, the nephew and niece of Trevor Hordley, at the memorial in Serifontaine commemorating the anniversary of the crash of their uncle's aircraft, 25 June 2013; At the scene of the crash are, from left to right, Peter Hordley, the farmer who witnessed the crash and rescued pieces of the aircraft, Pauline, and her husband Glyn; The original grave markers at Beauvais.

CHAPTER FIVE

THE SEVEN SOULS OF SIRACOURT

BY MARC HALL

A QUIET FRENCH VILLAGE NAMED SIRACOURT IN THE PAS DE CALAIS REGION HOUSED ONE OF MANY OF THE THIRD REICH'S V1 (VENGEANCE WEAPON) FLYING-BOMB FACILITIES. ON 6 JULY 1944 OPS WERE ON, AND A TOTAL OF 551 RAF BOMBER COMMAND AIRCRAFT TOOK TO THE AIR. ONE OF THE TARGETS WAS THE 'LARGE' SITE AT SIRACOURT, WHICH HAD BEEN SUBJECTED TO A HEAVY BOMBING RAID ONLY A WEEK PREVIOUSLY AND HAD ALREADY CLAIMED A NUMBER OF BOMBER CREW LIVES. IN THE EARLY HOURS OF THE MORNING OF 6 JULY, FLYING OFFICER BANNIHR AND HIS CREW OF NO. 424 SQUADRON WERE BRIEFED FOR THEIR TARGET AND MADE PREPARATIONS FOR WHAT WOULD UNKNOWINGLY BE THEIR LAST FLIGHT.

FLYING OFFICER BANNIHR had an experienced crew, most on their twenty-ninth operation and close to completing their first tour of operations. They had been flying together for approximately seven months, having received – at No. 1664 Heavy Conversion Unit – a glowing report: 'Above average pilot and good average crew. Competent navigator and bomb aimer, gunners above average.' The flight commander also mentioned: 'Above average Pilot. Steady and reliable with good crew co-ordination.' The original crew consisted of an air gunner by the name of Flight Lieutenant Melborn Leslie Mellstrom, DFC, who completed the conversion course with the other crew members. But on the day of the sortie, when the aircraft and crew were lost, Mellstrom was not on board and Flying Officer Viau had taken his place; it is not known why. Flight Lieutenant Mellstrom was later to lose his life just prior to the end of the war, on 10 April 1945, with No. 405 Squadron and now lies in the Berlin war cemetery. His DFC was awarded for flying forty-four operations against the enemy and he was lost in Lancaster ME315 after his turret was shot away by a German fighter that blew away his position and parts of the aircraft. The remainder of his crew made it back to the UK.

On the morning of 6 July 1944, the Bannihr crew left their base at RAF Skipton-on-Swale in Yorkshire

Left Alan May with his younger brother Robert and their mother Mabel. *Grant Bailey*

at 05.32, flying aboard Halifax LW169, bound for the large V1 bunker at Siracourt. They were expected back home in just a few hours. The lumbering Halifax roared down the runway and slowly climbed into clear conditions, heading for the target in northern France and the anti-aircraft fire that would shoot it from the sky. Exactly what occurred on board will never be known, but a number of other returning aircrews said that they believed they saw the aircraft go down, the Halifax hit by flak and spiralling slowly downwards. Although appearing momentarily to level out a short distance from the ground, it plunged to earth and exploded upon impact. During the descent it was believed one of the crew escaped as a parachute was seen to open. The eyewitnesses could not confirm it was this particular Halifax, but Bannihr's aircraft was the only one lost on the raid. The aircraft crashed at approximately 08.05 hours, leaving no survivors despite the parachute being observed, approximately 2 kilometres south of the town of Saint-Pol-sur-Ternoise, very close to the road that led to the town of Doullens. The town was located just 7 kilometres from the target. Seven families were now left without husbands and sons.

Left Alan May and his brother Robert. *Grant Bailey*

Right Navigator
Alan May on the left,
Air Gunner Stan
Queen on the right,
taken 1943.
*Grant Bailey and
Andrew Morrison*

In September 1944 German information was received via the Red Cross centre at Geneva that the Halifax was indeed shot down, with the loss of the crew. It showed that there was one unidentified airmen but that four others had been named, including May, Morrison, Viau and Bannihr. No mention was made of the remaining two missing airmen.

Subsequently, the task of solving this case was handed to Flight Lieutenant Milliard of No. 5 Section of the Missing Research and Enquiry Service (MRES), to make investigations – with what sketchy information was currently to hand – with the aim of locating the missing airmen. It proved to be a challenging case and the military cemetery at Saint-Pol was visited a number of times, with the initial visit in February 1945 by Flight Lieutenant Bugold. The mayor of the village was consulted and he supplied a map of the cemetery containing all of the burials for Allied personnel during the current conflict. The official records showed that five bodies of aircrew were laid to rest in the cemetery on 6 July 1944, four of which were not identified, but one having the number CAN.J22859 recorded. This service number related to the body of Flying Officer May. The remains were not recognisable and were brought to the cemetery by a German

Right Bannihr crew
Grant Bailey

warrant officer and two other ranks, and the cemetery keeper was only able to obtain the one service number. It was known that the aircraft had a crew of seven and that one parachute was seen, but despite enquires with the local population and Resistance no Allied airmen had been assisted around that time.

A further visit to the cemetery was made on 18 April 1945 and again the mayor of Saint-Pol was interviewed, who advised that the crew were killed by the impact. Flight Lieutenant Milliard was assured that the collective grave contained the bodies of all of the crew from the crashed Halifax, though unnamed in the records. It was also now said by the cemetery keeper that the Germans had recovered the bodies from the scene of the crash and handed them over to the cemetery completely stripped of all clothing and belongings, although this later proved to be unfounded. One other man was also spoken to and confirmed the bodies were from the crash site of this particular Halifax. He had been arrested on 8 October 1944 and found to be in possession of a Ronson cigarette lighter, which had belonged to Flying Officer Morrison, a gift that had been presented to the airman by the No. 8 Air Observer School in training. This was seized and returned to the family.

The cemetery held conflicting reports. Some showed that only five airmen were buried there, as per the initial visit. Further records suggested that three unknown airmen were buried on 6 July 1944, one of which was Canadian with the service number J22859 (Flying Officer May), and the remains of three more individuals were buried on 10 July, with the seventh, unknown, airman having no burial date shown.

Left A well worn picture of one of the crews Handley Page Halifax bombers
Grant Bailey and Andrew Morrison

This now made up the crew of seven, but there was no further information about the parachute that the other aircrews had seen. Local members of the population confirmed that it was not usually customary of the Germans to bury the dead on the same day and sometimes they left them for days or weeks before moving them and the wreckage. In this particular case, though, it seems to have been partially cleared on the same day as the crash. The later date of burial for three other airmen on 10 July was accounted for as their bodies had been removed from underneath the wreckage of the aircraft when this was taken away by the Germans. The last body was found sometime later and buried on the spot by a number of local people, later revealed to be Sergeant Dawson.

The investigation was closed temporarily, until it was time for the airmen to be made ready for their final identification and registration. However, in December 1945 further information had come to light from Lance Corporal Edwards, the step-brother of Sergeant Dawson. He stated that he had himself attended the cemetery and had dug up some of the graves for identification purposes without any formal permission. It was observed that some of the bodies were clothed and he thought he had confirmed the

grave of Sergeant Dawson as the body had sergeant stripes on the arms, and Dawson was the only sergeant in the crew at the time the aircraft was lost. Lance Corporal Edwards maintained that the story given to the investigating officer regarding the bodies being stripped naked had been untrue and that he had carried out his own investigations prior to the first official visit of Flight Lieutenant Milliard. It was then that an official exhumation was requested at the earliest opportunity to formally identify the bodies.

On 9 April 1947 Flight Lieutenant Milliard from the No. 5 Section of the MRES and Captain Hillier of the 83 Graves Concentration Unit, attended the military cemetery of Saint-Pol to exhume and identify the remains for their final burial. After consulting the cemetery records further, they made their way to row three located in the centre plot. The collective grave was then cleared and gradually the team dug down with their shovels and opened the grave up to reveal the remains of five intact bodies buried side by side, although they were beyond recognition. Mixed up in among these were a number of individual bones and scraps of clothing that appeared to be what survived of a sixth airman, which was not quite evident at the beginning of the exhumation.

The large bunker at Siracourt was easily identified by the Allies, the scale of construction is clear in the photograph on the left. The photograph on the right shows the devastation of the area after the attentions of Bomber Command in June and July 1944. The structure itself did not receive much severe damage owing to the thickness of the concrete walls and roof, however the bombing laid waste to the surrounding area and the Siracourt bunker failed to feature in the V1 offensive. *The National Archives and IWM CL 000280*

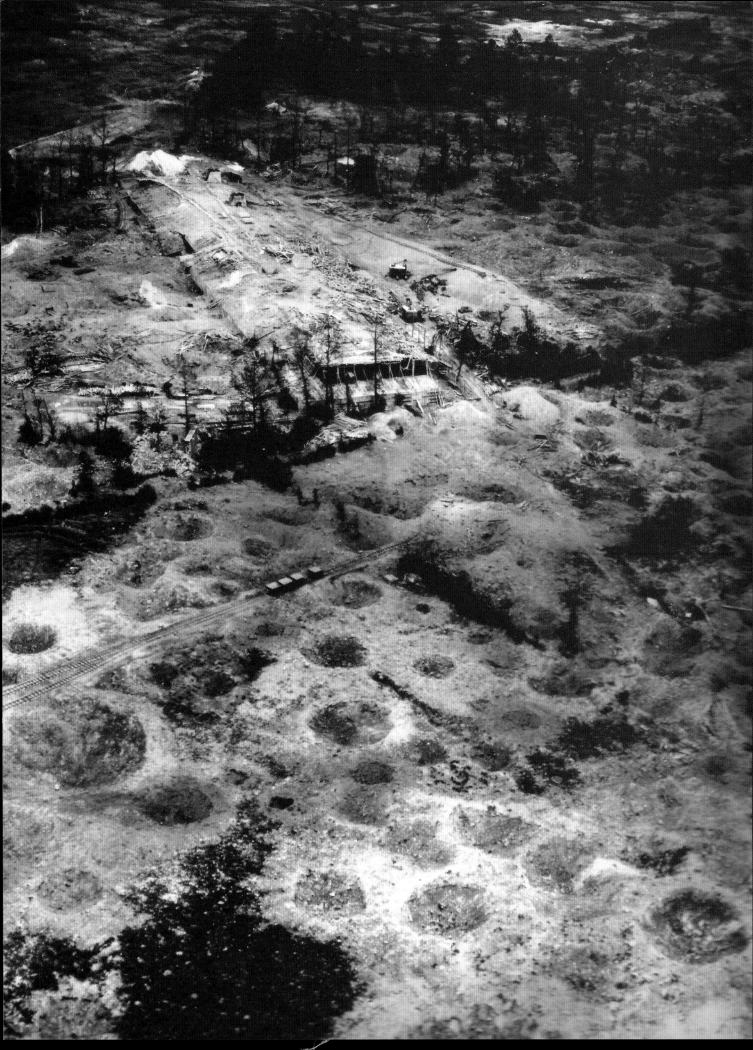

Starting from left to right, row three, grave one, the remains were positively identified as the pilot, a flying officer, having located a pilot's brevet and parts of a flying officer's braid and shirt. The second grave contained an airman identified by a laundry mark showing 859 on his clothing, believed to be the last three digits of Flying Officer May's service number, together with an electrically heated flying suit and aircrew sweater. The third and fourth graves held the remains of two flying officers, and items found with them included flying helmets with headphones, parachute harnesses and shirts. The fifth grave revealed an unknown airman, with scraps of clothing, and the

found near to the body addressed to Sergeant Dawson. Following the examination Dawson was removed and reburied inside the cemetery in his own grave. The remaining six aircrew were eventually registered and left as they were in a communal grave with only Flying Officer Morrison and Flying Officer May being positively identified.

The skipper in charge of the crew, Robert Huston Bannihr, also known as 'Bob', was one of the older members, born on 19 September 1920 in Detroit, Michigan, USA, and was the only American crew member on board the Halifax. Robert, named after

Left to right
Flying Officer Viau;
Walter Tomlinson;
Alan May;
Robert Bannihr;
Flying Officer Queen.
National archives of Canada

sixth grave contained remnants of clothing together with a number of bones, which were assumed to be the remains of the sixth airman.

It was the opinion of the investigating officer that the first three, in graves one to three, would be positively registered as individuals, while the others in graves four to six would have to be located in a communal grave upon registration. The seventh member of the crew was not located in the cemetery and was in fact buried on his own outside it, and it seems the reason for this was that he was found after the Germans had cleared the crash site of the remaining airman. He was buried on the spot where he was found by some local people, but was later moved to his present location following the liberation. It was assumed that the airman was Sergeant Dawson as the witness advised the investigating officer that an envelope was

his father, was the family's only son but there were also three sisters, one sadly not living at the time of enlistment.

Robert had a colourful background, having served previously in the US Navy Air Force as an aviation mechanic's mate, serving four years in San Diego, California. While there he was awarded a good conduct medal for his service. Having enlisted with the Navy since leaving school in 1937, and gaining mechanic qualifications, he was honourably discharged. Seemingly content with the military lifestyle, Robert wasted no time in volunteering for active service with the RCAF, having been previously instructed with air time on gunnery, flight engineer and mechanic duties. It was mentioned on his application form that he 'can do anything around a plane, except fly one'. The interviewing officer said he was the 'desirable type and above average American with a tall and slender build, clean, neatly dressed and pleasant manner'. His ambition following the end of the war was to return to school in order to study aircraft design or to continue a career in aviation.

Robert was accepted as a trainee pilot and began his initial training on the Tiger Moth aircraft at Belleville, Ontario, in 1942 and finally completed his service flying training on the Harvard, graduating with the award of his pilot wings in early 1943. It was not long before Robert was posted overseas where he joined No. 23 Operational Training Unit. While there, again he scored reasonably well in his exams but his

radio while growing up, as well as rugby and sailing. Walter wished to get into active service as soon as possible after leaving school, becoming part of the non-permanent active militia and serving in it for two years. It appears he also attempted to enlist with the Royal Canadian Engineers but his service lasted less than two months, as they had found out he was under the age of eighteen. Not to be downhearted he joined the Royal Canadian Navy Volunteer Reserve (RCNVR) on 17 June 1940 but shortly after, on 9 July 1940, Walter was given permission to join the RCAF. This transfer was approved on the grounds that immediate active service could not be promised to

instrument flying let him down a little, and although shown to be an energetic captain who led his crew well it was noted that slight distractions in the cockpit could divert his attention from flying. However, his ability in general, including his leadership qualities, improved following further experience. At the end of December 1943 the skipper and his crew were posted to No. 424 Squadron for operations and survived a little over seven months before all were killed.

Pilot Officer Walter Harold Tomlinson, the wireless operator on the crew, was twenty-three when he lost his life, born on 12 November 1921 in Kingston, Ontario. Both of his parents were actually English, his father Walter a soldier from Leeds and his mother Margaret from Burnley. Walter was their only child. He had a keen interest in model aeroplanes and amateur

him within the Navy. In November the RCAF interview observed him as 'quick minded, accurate and with a mature personality for his age', summing him up as an above average candidate all round. Following completion of his initial training in drill, signals and other core subjects, Walter was observed by the commanding officer to be 'a quiet airman who lacks dash and initiative. Reliable and dependable, although does not instil much confidence. Should improve with service and training.' A year later he enrolled at the No. 3 Wireless School and on successful completion he went on to his gunnery course. Walter arrived in the UK on 4 June 1943 and spent the next six months completing further training before finally being transferred for operational duties on 28 December 1943.

Flying Officer Alan Edward May was the aircraft's

navigator. He was one of two sons to Mabel and Edward May, and was born on 5 June 1922 in Winnipeg, Manitoba. Having completed his schooling in 1939, Alan took up temporary employment with a timber operator but left to attend United College and moved on to the University of Manitoba, graduating in 1941. Alan was of a heavy build and good physique, which reflected his hobbies as he enjoyed the physical sports of boxing, wrestling and rugby – team sports suited for the RCAF. Following nine months in the Canadian Officer Training Corps he enlisted with the RCAF on 13 November 1941 at the

flying. His flight training ceased on 23 May 1942; his report read: 'His over abundance of exuberance is perhaps one of his main faults. He flies as if every movement is something to be done forcefully and quickly – the idea that an aircraft might respond more readily to smooth and easy movements is one he finds impossible to put into execution. An excellent type of airman for any type of duty except precision work requiring patience.' Alan was remustered to a ground trade as a radio mechanic, but he was determined to make aircrew in some capacity and less than six weeks after leaving the flight school he enrolled on a navi-

Left Flying Officer Morrison; Initial grave marker. *National archives of Canada*

age of nineteen, with high hopes of becoming a pilot soon to be dashed. The interviewing officer was of the opinion that he suited the position of pilot or observer and was an 'exceptionally fine student and athlete with a good appearance and nice personality'.

The medical officer described Alan as 'alert, intelligent, cheerful and poised to do a good job but with a fiery character due to his father's war wounds'. The initial training began in March 1942 and went without a hitch – he was someone who had 'surplus energy and was burning with enthusiasm', as stated by his commanding officer. But his pilot training at the Elementary Flying Training School did not go to plan and he washed out before going solo. Despite strong motivation and high intellectual capacity, he could not grasp the concept of flying an aircraft, suffering from poor coordination and being too tense when

gators' course at Winnipeg, graduating in January 1943, achieving high marks in his practical work in the air and on the ground. Alan became operational on 28 December 1943 and had flown twenty-nine sorties at the time of his death at the age of twenty-two.

Flying Officer Raymond Gerald Viau was born on 29 September 1921 in Greenfield, Ontario. Another of the aircraft's air gunners, Raymond was somewhat suited for the role having been raised on a farm and hunting game since the age of twelve. His parents, Albert and Armancia, had a large family with a total of eight children, with Raymond one of the oldest siblings. He enlisted with the RCAF in the late summer of 1941, specifying ground duties, which are only shown on his service record as general duties. However, as the demand for aircrew increased, Raymond applied for remustering to aircrew and following an interview he was sent for training in June 1942. His interviewing officer described him as 'confident with a sincere manner, but quiet with an unassuming determination'.

Raymond commenced a gunnery course at the gunnery school in Mountain View, Ontario. The chief instructor commented that 'his air firing results were below average but he had no trouble in the class room and should make a good NCO'. Raymond passed his final exams and qualified on 25 September 1942, promoted to the rank of sergeant. Despite his quiet demeanour, Raymond did land himself in trouble on a number of occasions while serving, including being caught with others gambling in the classroom, and breaking out of the barracks just two days into a seven-day sentence of being confined to barracks. For these he received forfeiture in pay and further days in detention. Following his graduation a posting was then made overseas in late October 1942 to the UK, but it would be many months before he would see active service on operations, occupying his time with further gunnery training on air exercises around the UK until his final posting with No. 424 Squadron in November 1943.

Sergeant John Houseal Morrison was born on 16 August 1917 and was one of the oldest members of the crew, one of two sons to Bernard and Anna Morrison. John enlisted in Halifax, Nova Scotia, in June 1939. Patriotic to his country he clearly enjoyed the service lifestyle, noting on his application form: 'My ambition is to remain in the armed services and serve my country as best I can.' Upon enlistment he became a clerk but later transferred to begin flying training as a pilot. Despite his hard work, while at the Elementary Flying Training School he struggled with the grounding of the subject and would fly the aircraft by instinct rather than by the rules. His chief flying instructor commented that he 'lacked air sense and reacted too slowly to changing circumstances in the air'. On 7 July 1942 John was reprimanded for crashing an aircraft on his first solo flight after he raised the landing gear instead of the flaps. Following the request to discontinue pilot instruction, he was recommended to train as an air bomber and qualified in this on 22 January 1943. All of the remarks by the officers said he 'tried hard' and was 'keen and interested at all times'. Other comments included 'clean cut, bright worker, with

good leadership qualities, and officer type material'. At the time of his death he was an experienced airman; he had flown twenty-nine sorties over enemy territory, and was almost at the end of his first tour and set to enjoy a long period of leave away from operations.

Pilot Officer Stanley James Queen, another air gunner, was born in Colchester, Ontario, on 9 April 1921 and was one of two sons and a daughter to James and Mable Queen, although sadly both were deceased at the time he volunteered to go to war, leaving his sister as his next of kin. In spring 1942 Stanley made an application to the Navy for the position of ordinary seaman. In September of that year he was discharged at his own request, instead joining the air force to train as a pilot. The reason given for the transfer was that he wanted to get active and involved in the war, and it appeared the Navy was slow. He had volunteered his services for the duration of the war. There is, however, no record that he underwent any pilot training and the trade shown on official documents is for an air gunner only. Following completion of his gunnery course in June 1943 at Trenton, Stanley was posted to the processing depot located in Halifax, Nova Scotia, one of the main depots where trained aircrew would leave for the journey over to the UK. The class consisted of 122 pupils and Stanley excelled, obtaining third position in his class, and he was selected as a suitable candidate for a gunnery instructor should the position arise. The chief instructor commented that he 'displayed initiative and applies himself diligently'. And he had a 'sound knowledge of his trade; should make an excellent crew member'. Once in the UK he was crewed up and spent time with No. 23 Operational Training Unit and No. 1664 Heavy Conversion Unit before finally being posted to an operational squadron on 28 December 1943. On his death he left behind his sister and a wife named Stella whom he had married just a year previously in July 1943 at Windsor.

The flight engineer on board this Halifax was Sergeant Leonard Bert Dawson, and little is known about him. The only RAF member of the crew, he was assessed during training as accomplished and very keen, working well, with good results as a crew member. ●

CHAPTER SIX

WHAT PRICE A THIRD?

BY SEAN FEAST

IN THE LATE SPRING/EARLY SUMMER OF 1944, A DECISION WAS TAKEN SOMEWHERE IN THE HIGHER ECHELONS OF THE AIR MINISTRY TO 'CHANGE' THE WAY IN WHICH A TOUR OF BOMBER COMMAND OPERATIONS WAS TO BE MEASURED. THE TREND TOWARDS SHORTER, AND SEEMINGLY LESS DANGEROUS, TRIPS TO NORTHERN FRANCE IN SUPPORT OF THE PLANNED INVASION AND BEYOND MEANT THAT SUCH OPERATIONS WOULD NOT COUNT AS A FULL 'TRIP' BUT ONLY A FRACTION OF ONE – A THIRD. IT WAS ARGUED THAT SUCH FLIGHTS COULD NOT BE COMPARED TO THE LONG HAULS TO BERLIN OR STETTIN, AND SO PILOTS AND THEIR CREWS WOULD BE OBLIGED TO FLY MORE THAN THE 'STANDARD' TOUR OF THIRTY OPERATIONS BEFORE THEIR LIVES WOULD BE SPARED FOR A FEW BRIEF MONTHS WHILE THEY WERE 'RESTED'. FOR SOME, INCLUDING A YOUNG AUSTRALIAN FLIGHT LIEUTENANT PAUL SINCLAIR, DFC, AND HIS CREW, THE DECISION WAS TO HAVE FATAL CONSEQUENCES.

I N THE WINTER of 1943/44, the Battle of Berlin was in full swing. The commander-in-chief of Bomber Command, Arthur Harris, had assured his paymasters and the Prime Minister that he could smash the city from end to end, given the time and resources, and had set about proving his point. It was one of the bloodiest and deadliest periods in Bomber Command history, in which all of the major groups were involved, including the Halifax squadrons of No. 4 Group in the north, among them No. 76 Squadron at Holme-on-Spalding-Moor.

The squadron had a proud record, thanks in no small part to the leadership of one of its early commanding officers, Wing Commander Leonard Cheshire. (Cheshire later went on to be awarded the Victoria Cross for sustained gallantry.) By the end of 1943, with the second phase of the Battle of Berlin just beginning, Wing Commander Donald Smith, DSO, DFC, was in command. He in turn was 'screened' on 22 December, and Squadron Leader Iveson, who had started his operational career as a pilot officer on the squadron two years earlier, was promoted to wing commander and appointed officer commanding.

The squadron suffered its fair share of losses in those winter months, and new crews arrived to fill the gaps from various conversion units and other training establishments in the surrounding area. One of these new crews to arrive in October 1943 was led by a young Australian pilot, Paul Sinclair.

Sinclair was one of thousands of Commonwealth servicemen and women who answered the call to defend the mother country. A jackaroo on his father's sheep station at Moree in New South Wales, he had benefited from an independent school education, a factor that no doubt contributed to his later selection for a commission.

Enlisting in June 1941 at the age of nineteen, he had been awarded his flying badge a year later after training at 5 Elementary Flying Training School (5 EFTS) in Narromine and 1 Service Flying Training School (1 SFTS) at Point Cook. Embarking from Melbourne in November 1942, Pilot Officer Sinclair arrived in the UK in the New Year to continue his training in less benign surroundings than he had been used to 'down under'. The darkened skies of a blacked-out Britain held rather more danger to the novice pilot and required more specialist training. This took

place initially at an Advanced Flying Unit in Ramsbury (15 AFU), including a brief attachment to 1536 Beam Approach Training (BAT), and then at an Operational Training Unit (15 OTU) in Harwell to prepare for squadron life. It was at Harwell that he found himself a crew.

His crew comprised another Australian, and from his home state, Flight Sergeant Alexander Rodgers, RAAF. Rodgers, the air bomber, was the 'old man' of the crew at thirty, his pilot being only twenty-two. The remainder were all under twenty-five and included three Englishmen and two Welshmen: the flight

Left A former Jackaroo, Paul Sinclair developed into a first class pilot. *All photographs via Mike King.*

engineer Sergeant Ron Nevill, mid-upper gunner Flight Sergeant Fred Philips and wireless operator Sergeant Wilf Ray were all English; Flying Officer Gwynfor Watkins, the navigator, and Flight Sergeant David Blockley, the rear gunner, were Welsh.

Joining No. 76 Squadron from 1663 Conversion Unit (1663 CU), and having successfully negotiated the transition from the twin-engined Wellington to the four-engined Halifax, the crew were attached to C Flight and flew their first operation on the night of 20 January. It was a major raid on the German capital comprising almost 800 heavy bombers. And it was something of a sobering baptism of fire. For the squadron it was a maximum effort, but little went to plan. Of the twenty-four aircraft detailed, one failed to get off the ground, three returned early, and three

Right Paul Sinclair's crew from left to right: Watkins; Sinclair; Nevill; Rodgers; Blockley; Phillips; Ray.

Right Wilf Ray, the 22-year old wireless operator.

failed to return, two the victims of flak. The Sinclair crew, in a Halifax V, landed exhausted after a flight of almost eight hours, having arrived to find the target covered in cloud, and being obliged to bomb the estimated position of the sky markers.

Their difficult beginnings continued the next night with a planned attack on Magdeburg that went wrong from the beginning. The Halifax V of Flight Sergeant Eric Firth began to vibrate uncontrollably shortly after take-off, and the captain ordered the crew to abandon aircraft. They all got out safely with the exception of the pilot who was killed soon after when the aircraft exploded. He was not the only skipper killed that night. Some 57 aircraft were shot down out of an attacking force of 648 bombers – 8.8% of the total. Alarmingly, however, 35 of those knocked down were Halifaxes, 4 from Holme-on-Spalding-Moor. The squadron had lost 8 aircraft in less than 48 hours, including 3 pilots who had been with the squadron only a matter of weeks.

The Sinclair crew had its own brush with trouble while over the target area. David Blockley, in the rear turret, spotted a single-engined Bf 109 night fighter positioning itself for attack on the port quarter some 500 yards distant. As the enemy aircraft dived, Blockley called for his skipper to turn sharply to port, thus throwing off the fighter's aim. As the Halifax continued to turn, the German pilot was not able to press home his attack, but the crew could not relax, especially when another night fighter appeared almost dead astern. Now they had two night fighters to deal with. The first opened fire but missed, breaking off at about 250 yards on the port beam. Sinclair continued to throw the heavy bomber into a turn and suddenly, just as quickly as they appeared, the two fighters vanished. The Halifax continued on its bombing run, and the crew had the satisfaction of seeing their bombs hit the target. Fires could be seen

120 miles from the city on their return.

A two-week respite for the heavy bomber squadrons ended on 15 February with yet another attack on Berlin, this time involving the largest number of aircraft assembled to raid the German capital. The crews at No. 76 Squadron were in the process of replacing their disappointing Mk Vs with the more promising Halifax IIIs, and so only nine were required for that night's operation. One failed to return.

By the beginning of March, the squadron had been fully re-equipped, and the Sinclair crew took part in no fewer than six operations during the month, starting with an eight-hour trip to Stuttgart. They went back to Stuttgart two weeks later (15 March) on their return from seven days' leave and were attacked by a night fighter head-on. The first that Sinclair knew of the night-fighter's presence was when he saw a burst of tracer fire go over his head. The deadly baubles of flame seemed to accelerate as they neared the cockpit; he ducked instinctively and pushed the control column forward to put the aircraft into a straight dive. The assault was over in a flash and no damage was reported. It had, nonetheless, been a terrifying experience.

The raid on Stuttgart was followed by operations to Frankfurt (18 and 22 March), Berlin (24 March) and Essen (26 March). During the strike on Berlin they overshot the target and were unable to regain the bomber stream, dropping bombs on a secondary target near Jüterbog instead. The trip to Essen was similarly disappointing, as some way into the flight they lost their starboard inner engine and were obliged to chalk up an early return. The month ended with the attack on Nuremberg, a calamitous night for Bomber Command and a memorable raid for Paul Sinclair and David Blockley.

The squadron detailed seventeen aircraft for the attack but in the event only fourteen took off and that number was reduced shortly after when another Halifax was forced to return with engine trouble. Of the thirteen who proceeded to the target, three failed to return, including the C Flight commander, Squadron Leader Kenny Clack, DFM. (Clack was on his second tour.) It might have been more. The air gunners within the crew of Flight Lieutenant Bolt fought off an assault from a Messerschmitt Bf 210 night fighter, and believed they shot it down. A single-engined fighter also attacked Halifax M-Mother,

with Paul Sinclair at the controls. The combat report tells its own story:

The tail gunner sighted a single engine fighter which he later identified as an Me109 [sic] on the port quarter slightly above, range 500 yards. He warned the pilot to prepare to do a diving turn to port. The fighter was then seen to come into the attack, dead astern, slightly above, and when it was at a range of 400 yards, the gunner ordered the pilot to carry out the combat manoeuvre 'Corkscrew go' and this was carried out by the pilot starting to port. As the fighter closed in to 300 yards it opened fire at the Halifax and at the same moment, the gunner opened fire at the fighter which only gave one burst, the trace from which was seen to pass below the Halifax. The tail gunner fired two bursts at the fighter and during the second one, he held the fighter in the centre of his cone of fire and is therefore certain that he was able to score quite a number of strikes.

Due to the 'corkscrew' manoeuvre taken, the gunner was unable to say for certain in which direction the enemy fighter broke off the attack but just as the gunner had given 'resume course go' both he and the mid upper gunner and the engineer saw what they took to be a rocket dead astern, slightly above, coming down to dead astern, level. It seemed to hover in this position for a second and was then seen to dive straight down through the cloud and explode on the ground. Although the three members of the crew who saw this burning object thought at first that it was a rocket, they are convinced that it was the fighter with whom they had the combat and therefore claim this ME109 as destroyed. The visibility at the time was very clear with a bright moon almost dead astern.

David Blockley fired off some 700 rounds and might have fired more had not three of the guns failed during the second burst. Here his hours of training at air gunnery school (5 AGS) kicked in and he cleared the stoppages in case of further attack. They landed back at base none the worse for their encounter.

Their actions drew the attention of the commanding officer of No. 76 Squadron, Wing Commander Douglas Iveson ('Hank' Iveson won the DSO, DFC and Bar during the war; his son, a Harrier pilot, was shot down during the Falklands conflict and survived). Iveson recommended both men for a gallantry award, the Distinguished Flying Cross for the pilot, and the Distinguished Flying Medal for his air gunner, the citation stating that both men had displayed 'much skill and excellent co-operation' and proved themselves to be 'valiant members of the aircraft's crew'. (An abridged version of the citation appeared in the London Gazette on 5 May.)

After the debacle of the Nuremberg attack in which Bomber Command lost almost 100 aircraft in a single night, the main force squadrons were stood down to 'make do and mend', and to allow new crews to be brought up to scratch. It was not until 9 April (by which time Paul had been promoted to flight lieutenant) that Sinclair and his crew were called for action: an assault on Lille. Bomber Command was tasked with operations in support of the imminent invasion of Europe and the opening of a second front, attacking a range of different targets such as vital communication links; railway marshalling yards; locomotive sheds; coastal batteries; troop concentrations; and ammunition dumps. To maintain the pretence of an invasion in the Pas de Calais, the bombers were obliged to strike at targets all along the French coast, to keep the Germans guessing. Sinclair took part in raids against Villeneuve St Georges (26 April), Montzen (27 April), Achères (30 April), Malines (1 May), Mantes Gassicourt (6 May) and Hasselt (12 May). Further ops followed against Cherbourg (1 June) and Trappes (2 June) before D-Day, 6 June, when the squadron mounted an attack on Montfleury, bombing a series of gun positions through heavy cloud.

These were indeed shorter trips – typically four hours in duration – but the dangers were still very real. A raid on 22 April (the Sinclair crew were on leave) resulted in the loss of two senior pilots: Squadron Leader Stan Somerscales, DFC, and Flight Lieutenant Reginald Lemmon. Somerscales had only recently taken over as C Flight commander following the death of Kenny Clack. His place was taken by Squadron Leader Nathaniel Shove, DFC, a second-tour man who was himself shot down and killed over Hasselt as navigator within the crew of Flying Officer Jack Newcombe. Flak and fighters did not appear to discriminate as to whom they shot down or how far they had flown to meet their fate.

There were other dangers too. On the attack on Malines, Sinclair's air bomber, Alexander Rodgers, reported that one of the 1,000-lb bombs had 'hung up' and failed to release. It was some way from the target before the crew were finally able to jettison the bomb 'safely'. They were fortunate. It had been known for aircraft to return to base with a bomb still on board, and for that bomb to shake loose and explode upon landing.

The Sinclair crew flew nine operations in June, all in support of the invasion, and the squadron lost one of its number on the night of 7/8 June, two on 12/13 June (one of which was struck by a bomb dropped from above), and two more on the night of 22/23 June, including the aircraft of yet another senior officer, Squadron Leader Bob West, RCAF. West was the commander of A Flight. On an attack on Blainville at the end of the month, and yet another 'easy' trip, the squadron lost three aircraft in a single night. And it could have been many more; four other aircraft reported combats with night fighters.

A new menace that required the attentions of Bomber Command in the summer of 1944 was the dreaded V1 – the flying bomb whose launch sites and storage facilities had been identified throughout northern France and in range of London. Paul Sinclair – now one of the most experienced pilots in the squadron – flew five operations in the first half of July to Saint-Martin-l'Hortier, Croix-d'Alle, Château Benapré, Nucourt and Manneville; it might have been six, other than for a faulty engine caused by excessive oil temperature that prevented him taking off for a raid on Thiverny on the 12th.

A week later he found himself on the battle order for an attack on the flying bomb launching site in Acquet, to the north-east of Abbeville. It was to be a small raid involving sixty-two aircraft, with the target marked by Pathfinder Mosquitoes and Lancasters. The Sinclair crew were one of twenty-four detailed from No. 76 Squadron; Halifax aircraft from No. 78 Squadron made up most of the remainder.

The assault was to take place in the small hours of the morning of 19 July. Sinclair, in Halifax LK873, S-Sugar, took off at 22.08 hours, one of the first of twenty-three squadron aircraft that would eventually get off the ground. The bombers crossed the enemy coast shortly after 00.20 hours and reached the target ten minutes later at 00.30, peering through the gloom at the red target indicators that marked the objective. They listened, too, for the voice of the master bomber for further instructions but nothing was heard until after their bombs had fallen.

In the darkness, the rear gunner in another C Flight Halifax – T-Topsy, flown by one of No. 76 Squadron's Norwegian pilots, 'Carl' Larsen – saw fiery beads of tracer darting across the sky, and then an explosion as they appeared to find their target, and a bomber began to fall to earth. The navigator in Topsy noted the exact time in his log and one of the gunners continued to look for parachutes, and other fighters. The tragedy would have been seen by other aircrew and details compared at debriefing. The victim was S-Sugar. After the war it would be established that Sinclair's vanquisher was an ace pilot, the commander (Staffelkapitan) of 8./NJG5 – Oberleutnant Werner Hopf. Hopf claimed a Halifax III at 00.32 hours in the Amiens area. He claimed another shortly after (a No. 78 Squadron aircraft flown by thirty-year-old warrant officer George Stratford) for his tenth and eleventh kills. (Hopf survived the war, and is reported to have escaped to Switzerland on 30 April 1945.)

When it hit the ground, the Halifax disintegrated. Had anyone survived the initial engagement, they would have been killed instantly by the impact. Parts of aircraft and its crew were scattered over a wide area. A subsequent investigation found a map with the name 'Sinclair' written upon it – a poignant remnant identifying what was left of the pilot and his crew.

Paul Sinclair was remembered by his contemporaries as a quite outstanding pilot, and thought of by his parents as a beloved only son who died nobly – the memory inscribed on his gravestone. His squadron commander, 'Hank' Iveson, described him in his letter to Paul's parents as 'one of our very best pilots … who could be depended upon in an emergency'. At the time of his death he had successfully completed at least thirty operations. The attack on Acquet was the thirty-first with his crew. The aircraft came down at Sailly-Flibeaucourt in the Department of the Somme. The crew is buried in a collective grave in the Sailly-Flibeaucourt churchyard, and their names are also recorded in a book of remembrance in the Church of All Saints, Holme-on-Spalding-Moor, along with the 800 other aircrew who gave their lives

flying with No. 76 Squadron between June 1941 and April 1945.

'Bert' Kirtland, DFC, the long-time honorary secretary of the No. 76 Squadron Association, was friends with Sinclair's wireless operator, Wilf Ray. They had joined the squadron at much the same time, and flown roughly the same number of trips. He recalls:

When we started our tour we expected to do 30 Operations – not many did, but you always thought that you would make it. You had to think that.

About the time of D-Day, Bomber Command 'moved the goalposts' as it were. Someone in Command ruled that the short sorties about that time should not count as a full trip and a 'points' system was introduced which none of us understood. What we did understand was that we continued operating after our 30th trip.

Acquet was our 33rd trip and it was probably about the same for Wilf Ray's crew. In the week following Acquet we did two more trips – back on strategic targets – Bottrop in the Ruhr and Kiel. On the 25 July after the Kiel raid we were 'screened'. Had Sinclair's crew got back from Acquet that fateful night they were perhaps one or two trips from finishing their tour.

'Bert' Kirtland says that it was a cruel twist of fate that finally did for this gallant airman and his crew: 'It should have been an easy one for an experienced crew but they just ran out of luck.' ●

CHAPTER SEVEN

MASTER OF THE SKY

BY SEAN FEAST

ASK ANY OF THE VETERANS OF NOS 109 AND 582 SQUADRONS AT LITTLE STAUGHTON
WHAT THEY THOUGHT OF 'HEAVY OBOE' OPERATIONS, AND THE ANSWER IS LIKELY TO BE
BLUNT. INTENDED TO BRING PINPOINT ACCURACY ON EVEN THE SMALLEST OF TARGETS,
THEY WERE THE IDEAL METHOD OF HITTING THE V1 LAUNCHING SITES. IN THEORY. IN
PRACTICE, HOWEVER, THEY COULD HAVE DEADLY CONSEQUENCES FOR THE BRAVE MEN
OF PATHFINDER FORCE (PFF).

IT WAS ANOTHER bright and sunny summer's day in northern France. The Met men had forecast cloud over the target, a V1 launching site in the Forêt du Croc, about ten miles from Dieppe. But they had been wrong; their predictions were never 100% accurate, but they did their best.

The attack planned for 20 July 1944 was to come in two waves of ten aircraft each. This was an unusual raid, almost experimental. Avro Lancasters made up the bulk of the force, including one in the second wave that was equipped with a precision blind-bombing device known as 'Oboe'. Oboe was a technology more usually installed in fast-flying Mosquitoes and accurate to within yards, not miles. It required the navigator to listen to a series of signals transmitted to the aircraft to enable it to fly along an imaginary 'beam'. When it dropped its bombs, others would follow. But there was a drawback to Oboe. It meant flying straight and level over the target area, and the signal could be easily lost. Which meant things could go wrong. And they did.

The leader of the first wave, struggling with a poor beam signal, abandoned the attack while still some way short of the target, and led the first formation away. The second wave – with an Oboe-equipped Lancaster in the vanguard – pressed on, determined to carry out their duty. The Germans were by now alive to the dangers, and the flak battery at Arques-la-Bataille soon had their range. Flak peppered the sky, striking the lead Lancaster, which started to burn. The aircraft behind was also hit, and reared alarmingly. Bombs were inadvertently dropped, but too early.

The pilot of the Oboe Lancaster, Squadron Leader James Foulsham, DFC, AFC, had only moments to live.

James (Jim) Foulsham was born into a generation that was fascinated by flying, and was delighted in October 1935 when he was granted a Short Service Commission in the RAF as an acting pilot officer. The youngest of three children, he had enlisted shortly after his older brother, Bill, although their careers would follow very different paths.

'Freddie', as he was known by his service friends, learned to fly at 6 Flying Training School (6 FTS) at Netheravon in Wiltshire, and upon being awarded his wings eventually found himself at No. 57 Squadron, piloting first the Hawker Hind and soon after

the Bristol Blenheim twin-engined light bomber. It was in many respects a 'plum' posting, flying one of the fastest bombers of its time, and it was not long before his peacetime training was put to the test for real with the declaration of war on 3 September 1939. Within days the squadron – designated a 'strategic reconnaissance' squadron and under the command of Wing Commander Harry 'Wings' Day – was ordered to France, Freddie flying one of the squadron's aircraft (Blenheim L1143) to Roye to become part of the RAF component of the British Expeditionary Force (BEF). Strategic reconnaissance (Strat.R) sorties were dangerous affairs. Single aircraft would fly to an advanced air base closer to the German border, refuel, and then head off to reconnoitre a particular part of the Siegfried Line. They had to photograph anything of interest – troop movements, vehicle convoys, ammunition dumps etc. – and then return to Roye or indeed any one of a number of UK RAF stations if deemed prudent to do so.

The first Strat.R sorties were little short of a disaster, the squadron commander being lost on his very first operation, and another squadron character, Mike Casey, following shortly afterwards. (Mike Casey was shot as one of the 'fifty' following the Great

Right The Foulsham family in 1933. Brother Bill (left) won the Military Cross in Palestine.

Escape in 1944.) Fighters were the main problem; however fast their little Blenheims could fly, the Bf 109s were quicker and more deadly.

Somewhat chastened by their experiences, the squadron continued to operate under a new CO, Squadron Leader (later Wing Commander) Arthur Garland, while their losses mounted.

This was the period known as the 'phoney war', though there was nothing phoney about losing friends and comrades. Freddie waited until 3 December before being called to fly his first operation, a Strat.R of north-west Germany. He opted to return to Honington after a trip of some four and a half hours – an apparently wasted flight as it happens, for the camera froze and no photographs were taken.

The first few weeks of 1940 were punctuated by flying training, lectures and the occasional squadron sortie. They also began to re-equip with the Blenheim Mk IV, and on 11 March Freddie was appointed acting flight lieutenant, unpaid. The Operations Record Books for that period are somewhat incomplete, but it appears that Freddie flew a Strat.R on 16 March, flying on to the UK for he returned the next day with a brand new Mk IV (L6811). He certainly flew a two-hour visual reconnaissance sortie on 19 March and returned to the advanced field at Metz without incident.

The phoney war became real with the invasion of the Low Countries in May 1940, and Freddie soon found himself in the thick of the action. On 17 May, he attacked an armoured column in the morning and flew an armed reconnaissance later that same day. That evening the squadron was obliged to abandon its airfield in the face of the advancing Wehrmacht. Three days later they were back in the UK, bruised and battered by their encounter, and having had to leave much of their equipment behind.

From Hawkinge, the squadron continued to operate, Freddie flying one last reconnaissance on 24 May before the squadron was withdrawn to re-equip and resupply. They did not begin operating again until July, by which time the squadron had relocated to Lossiemouth in the north of Scotland in the company of No. 21 Squadron as a counter to the build-up of German forces in Norway.

There was no respite. On the morning of 9 July, the two squadrons were briefed for an attack on the airfield at Stavanger. Freddie, recently promoted to squadron leader, was leading one of two sections of No. 57 Squadron. It was a total disaster. Over the target the formation was met by flak and fighters and in short order no fewer than seven Blenheims were shot down, including Pilot Officer Richard Hopkinson and Sergeant Frank Mills and their crews from No. 57 Squadron, lost without trace. A third Blenheim from No. 57, flown by Flight Lieutenant John Hird, was also severely damaged. The officer commanding No. 21 Squadron, 34-year-old Wing Commander Leslie Bennett, similarly failed to return.

At the end of 1940, Freddie was attached to the Blind Approach School before being posted to RAF Wyton in 1941 to undertake aircraft ferrying duties. He travelled twice by sea to Canada and on to the United States with his crew to fly Lockheed Hudson and Boeing Flying Fortress aircraft back to the UK.

Familiar now with flying aircraft with four engines, in the autumn of 1941 he was posted to No. 15 Squadron, operating the Short Stirling, the first of the RAF's four-engined 'heavies'. An operation on 14 August nearly ended in disaster when he could not get his wheels up on take-off, after which his port inner engine lost power. Jettisoning his bombs and fuel he successfully crash-landed near Ramsey.

He had similar misfortune during a planned raid on Berlin on 2 September when again he was forced to abandon the attack on the primary target when the port inner packed up. Searching for a suitable secondary target he was thwarted by cloud, and was forced to offload his bombs in the sea. His run of bad luck continued the following week with his first raid on Italy, when a mix-up in communications prompted him to return home, his duty not carried out.

Rested from operations, Freddie was posted to 7 Flying Instructors School (7 FIS) from where he arrived to assume command of 1524 Beam Approach Training (BAT) Flight at RAF Newton in May 1942. He took charge of the Central Navigation School the following year, being awarded the Air Force Cross (AFC) in the New Year's Honours of 1944, the citation stating: 'This officer has been in charge of flying at the Central Navigation School for the past five months. In addition to the time spent flying, instructing and testing new equipment, Squadron Leader Foulsham has reorganized the whole flying section and brought it to a high state of efficiency.' At the time of his award, he had accumulated some 2,140 hours of flying.

With his work at the Central Navigation School completed, Freddie was posted to 1655 Mosquito Training Unit based at Marham in Norfolk, to learn how to fly 'the wooden wonder' – the De Havilland Mosquito. The unit was part of 8 Group, training new pilots and navigators for operations within Pathfinder Force (PFF). Part of this training included instruction on the use of Oboe, the blind-bombing device that was proving to be unerringly accurate, and giving further 'edge' to Bomber Command attacks.

At Marham, Freddie was paired with a second tour navigator, Flying Officer John Swarbrick. It was a happy union based on mutual respect. John, who was comparatively old for aircrew, had completed a tour of thirty-one operations with No. 115 Squadron while still a sergeant. 'Rested' and commissioned, he arrived at 1655 MTU via 2 School of Air Navigation and 29 Operational Training Unit (29 OTU).

After six weeks familiarising themselves with their aircraft and PFF techniques, Freddie and John were posted to No. 109 Squadron on 17 February 1944 to commence a second tour. A Pathfinder tour comprised forty-five operations as opposed to the standard thirty required within a main force squadron. But the benefits included enhanced pay and accelerated promotion, assuming they lived that long.

The squadron to which they were posted was one of only two Oboe-equipped target-marking units, the other being No. 105 Squadron based at Bourn. It had already achieved outstanding success during the Battle of the Ruhr, and rejoiced in its squadron motto Primi Hastati – The first of the Legion. Their arrival coincided with the appointment of a new officer

Left Foulsham at No. 6 FTS, Netheravon.

commanding, Wing Commander Richard Cox, AFC, although he too was replaced in May by a Canadian, Wing Commander George Grant, DSO, DFC (and later Bar to his DSO).

Freddie and John's first Mosquito sortie took place on 1 March but proved something of an anticlimax when the bomb doors failed to open. Their Oboe equipment let them down on the following night, obliging them to bomb on dead reckoning (DR). It was third time lucky on 7 March, with a successful attack on Krefeld that presaged a run of better fortune for the remainder of the month, which was only spoiled by further technical failures over Florennes (18 March) and Laon (23 March). On the latter, they brought their bombs and target indicators home with them, following orders from the PFF chief (Air Vice Marshal Donald Bennett) that no markers were to be dropped unless the navigator was completely sure of his target.

A study of Freddie's forty-two Mosquito operations suggests that there were twenty-two successful releases and a further seven occasions where their bombs were dropped on DR or released in salvo with other aircraft. On three trips they were flying in reserve, and their marking was not required, and on ten occa-sions their duty was not carried out, either as a result of technical failure or defeat for other reasons.

One of their finer trips was marking the gun batteries at Merville on the night of 5 June 1944, in advance of the invasion of Europe (D-Day) that took place only hours later. The guns covered Sword beach, and it was vital that they were taken out. In the event, although the marking was accurate the bombs missed the target, and the guns were disabled in a heroic action soon after by the 9th Parachute Battalion – an attack that has gone down in legend.

On 2 April, the squadron moved to Little Staughton in Bedfordshire to 'share' with a newly formed heavy bomber unit, No. 582 Squadron. The 'new' squadron had been created by hiving off flights from two different squadrons – Nos 7 and 156 – thus giving them a nucleus of men and machines to which further crews and aircraft were subsequently added to bring them up to full strength.

The logic of 'twinning' a Mosquito squadron with a 'heavy' squadron was an obvious one and led to some healthy rivalries that only very occasionally spilled over into something more. But for the main part, the crews lived and worked together happily, and this 'closeness' was to be tested in the fire when

Right 'Freddie' Foulsham (circled) at No. 1524 BAT Flight, March 1943.

attacks on the German battleship *Scharnhorst* in June. He was awarded the Distinguished Flying Cross (DFC) again, unusually, for a successful attack on a German U-boat (submarine) the following month, his citation declaring that he had completed no fewer than ninety-two operations over the sea, from

assumed command of Weightman's aircraft and crew.

The best description of what happened next is told by Flying Officer Jeff Chapman. He was the wireless operator in the crew of Flight Lieutenant Gerry O'Donovan (later DSO, DFC), a very experienced Pathfinder who was flying just behind the leader in

Left The crew in 1943, from left to right, Reg MacArthur, Graham Aungiers, James Gresty, Edgar Pratt, Tom Bower.

maritime reconnaissance to strikes against enemy shipping. Rested from operations he spent more than three years in various training and instructor roles, before at last returning to the fight with No. 582 Squadron and rapidly becoming a 'master bomber' – the elite of the elite.

The nine aircraft of No. 582 Squadron aircraft took off from Little Staughton a little after 14.20 hours; nothing happened on their journey out to suggest the tragedy that would unfold, although the lack of cloud cover was a little disconcerting. All went well until it was time for the Oboe run of the lead Mosquito in the first wave, flown by Flight Lieutenant Ken Wolstenholme, DFC (later of World Cup fame). Wolstenholme was unable to acquire the signal satisfactorily, and was obliged to abandon the attack, which he signified by the firing of a red Very cartridge and leading the first wave of Lancasters away from the target to allow the second wave a clear run. Now it was Foulsham and Swarbrick's turn, having

the second wave. They had been practising close formation flying in daylight for some weeks, and now it was time to try it for real:

We were going in to attack in a twin line-astern formation with slight variation in height to avoid the slipstream of the aircraft in front. We were in the second aircraft and flying about 15 to 20 feet above the leader with our port wing just over and slightly behind his starboard wing.

The leader opened his bomb doors; we opened ours and so on down the line. It would be about 30 seconds to the drop. I was standing up next to my seat with my head in the astrodome and could see it all: the leader [Foulsham/Swarbrick] just slightly below us and others staggered at different heights behind, each swaying slightly as in some slow, macabre elephantine dance in the sky – sinister yet fascinating to watch. It was a perfectly clear day and I felt reasonably comfortable with our situation. If fighters attacked they would get a rough

Right John Weightman at No. 3 FTS.

Right John Weightman, awarded the DFC after more than 90 operations.

time from a total of 120 Browning machine guns each firing 1,000 rounds per minute!

And then it happened. One did not usually hear the bursts of flak above the roar of the engines. If one did, then it was very close indeed. We heard this one. A 'whoof' and a ball of flame, instantly gone as we flew through it. Our aircraft was spattered with small bits of exploding shell, some of which went clean through us and out the other side, filling the fuselage for the moment with a cloud of pulverized aluminium dust. One piece on its way through tore the sleeve of my flying jacket.

The port wing of the leading aircraft, however, was a mass of flame which streamed back as far as the tailplane in the slipstream having, I judged, received a direct hit on or near the port inner engine or one of the fuel tanks. It was obvious they would have to bale out, and quickly, if they were to survive.

I saw a face in the astrodome, no doubt the wireless op, and the rear and mid upper gunners looking from their turrets and the blazing wing. The leader kept on, straight and level, waiting for the electronic signal to drop his bombs, still with some 20 seconds to go. After what seemed like another very long 10 seconds the whole of the port wing folded upwards at a right angle and completely broke off, the aircraft turning on its back and [going] into a crazy downward gyration. I watched it for some time. I saw no parachutes open and did not expect to; centrifugal forces would see to that.

When the shell burst our flight engineer, who was stretched out horizontally in the nose with his eyes glued to the open bomb bay of the leader, was temporarily blinded and because his thumb was hovering over the bomb release 'tit', inadvertently pressed it. The rest of the gaggle behind us saw our bombs fall away and let go their own. Down went the whole lot, missing the target by at least a mile.

None of us spoke and it was the skipper's somewhat measured 'course for home please, navigator' that broke the silence.

Another eyewitness was John Torrans, flight engineer in the crew of Squadron Leader Bob Wareing, DFC and Bar: 'We were flying on his [Weightman's] starboard at about 16,000ft over France when his aircraft was hit by anti-aircraft fire. Fuel and smoke started to emit from the port wing trailing edge. We immediately called him on R/T to inform him of this damage. There was a large flash and an explosion, and the aircraft just disintegrated and all that was left was a large black cloud.'

Tommy MacLachlan, a decorated air gunner flying with Pilot Officer Joe Street also witnessed the drama unfold: 'The leading aircraft was only a hundred yards ahead from our port side. As the mid upper gunner (Reg MacArthur) waved to me the Lancaster's port wing broke off and the aircraft went straight down and I saw it crash in a wood.'

Disaster had struck. Foulsham's aircraft had been fatally hit, and the formation behind had all dropped their bombs short in the mistaken belief that the signal had been given. For a few brief moments, Foulsham's Lancaster continued on its run, and successfully released its bombs before falling out of the sky. There were no survivors from the crash that resulted. DFCs for Foulsham and Swarbrick were gazetted soon after their deaths. Both men arguably deserved more.

Jim Foulsham kept a diary during his time in the RAF. The last entry at the end of a short period of leave in July 1944 was to express satisfaction with his painting of a pram awaiting the birth of his daughter, Shirley, the child he was never to see.

In the summer of 2014, seventy years after the tragedy, families gathered to see Jim's daughter unveil a memorial to the men killed that day at Freulleville, where the crew had originally been buried before being reinterred at the Dieppe Canadian War Cemetery at Hautot-sur-Mer. Jim's grandsons wore his medals with great pride. The splendid granite memorial is a fitting tribute to a heroic action. ●

Clockwise from left
The memorial stone in Freulleville Churchyard. 'In memory of those who died at Manoir du Val that day in the service of their country'; The original cross marking the graves of James Foulsham, John Swarbrick, Graham Aungiers and Tom Bower; James Foulsham's DFC and AFC; Foulsham's father and Stella, Jim's widow, outside Buckingham Palace.

CHAPTER EIGHT

FRIENDLY FIRE

BY ROBERT OWEN

IN THE FIRST TWO WEEKS OF JULY 1944 THE RAF'S HEAVY BOMBERS CARRIED OUT PARTICULARLY ACCURATE AND EFFECTIVE ATTACKS ON THE V1 SUPPLY DEPOTS AT SAINT-LEU-D'ESSERENT AND NUCOURT. THE GERMANS RESPONDED AND MADE ALTERATIONS TO THEIR SUPPLY SYSTEM, BUT ALLIED INTELLIGENCE WATCHED CLOSELY AND IT SOON BECAME CLEAR TO THE ALLIES THAT THE RAILWAY TUNNEL AT RILLY-LA-MONTAGNE WAS BEING USED TO STORE FLYING BOMBS. THIS TUNNEL HAD TO BE SEALED, WITH BOMBER COMMAND TASKED TO CAVE IN THE ENTRANCES.

AS THE V-WEAPON offensive gained momentum, demands increased for both Bomber Command and the US 8th Air Force to destroy the increasing numbers of launching sites being identified. This would require considerable resources; the sites were small and well camouflaged against attack, their construction and dispersal mitigated against bomb damage. However, by the end of June sufficient intelligence had been assembled to formulate a new policy intended to limit the number of enemy weapons available to fire.

There was insufficient information to identify and strike at all the factories manufacturing these weapons. In any case, production was bound to be dispersed, creating a similar problem to the launch sites. However, it was soon realised that rather than having stockpiles of weapons at the launching sites, completed V1s were being dispatched initially to a small number of rear storage depots at the rate of about fifty a day. The flying bombs were then checked and allocated to individual launching sites in sufficient quantities to maintain the desired rate of fire. The storage depots presented a potential choke point. If these could be attacked and put out of action the Germans would not only be denied large quantities of completed weapons, but they would be forced to devise a new means of supply, placing even greater strain on already stretched logistics and transport.

Accordingly, on 1 July 1944 the 'Crossbow' target schedule was revised and priority placed on the storage depots, notably the site at Saint-Leu-d'Esserent, in the valley of the River Oise, 20 miles north of Paris, where a limestone quarry, latterly used for growing mushrooms, was being used as underground storage. By 25 July successful assaults against the Saint-Leu and another dump at Nucourt resulted in the focus being switched to a further V1 depot at Rilly-la-Montagne, 6 miles south of Reims. Here the Germans had reduced a 2-mile-long twin-track railway tunnel to single-track operation to create storage space. Officially designated as Feldmulag (Feldmunition-lager/ Field Munition Depot) 1116, the Germans also gave it the code name 'Richard'. Air Marshal Sir Arthur Tedder ordered that this should now be designated primarily as a target for the US 8th Air Force. However, perhaps not surprisingly in view of the outstanding success achieved against the Saumur railway tunnel

shortly after D-Day, it was also agreed that the tunnel's two entrances should be targeted by No. 617 Squadron with 'Tallboy' bombs.

Rilly was first attacked on 17 July 1944, when 58 B-24 Liberators from the 2nd and 3rd Bomb Divisions, USAAF, dropped 198 tons of bombs, causing extensive damage to the track, to both north and south tunnel entrances and to property in the village itself. Although a successful raid, it was estimated that the damage would not take long to repair, particularly at the northern entrance. By 25 July Rilly was once more the priority storage depot target and on 31 July No. 5 Group Headquarters issued orders for a further strike.

Among the crews who were to be detailed for this operation was that of Flight Lieutenant Bill Reid, VC. Although only on his first tour Reid, a 22-year-old Glaswegian with 24 operations to his credit, was the holder of the country's highest award for gallantry: the Victoria Cross.

Reid's award had been gained during his tenth operation, on the night of 3 November 1943, when serving with No. 61 Squadron. Outbound to Düsseldorf his Lancaster was attacked first by a Bf 110 and later by an Fw 190. Although badly wounded, with his navigator killed and aircraft badly damaged, Reid had pressed on and bombed the target, bringing his aircraft home to a crash-landing at the USAAF base at Shipdham. After a period of convalescence Reid had been summoned to see Air Vice Marshal Sir Ralph Cochrane, AOC No. 5 Group, who told him that he was being posted to No. 617 Squadron. Flying Officer Reid, VC, arrived on 13 January 1944, shortly after the squadron had transferred from Coningsby to Woodhall Spa.

Left
Bill Reid and Les Rolton in the summer of 1944. Behind them the terrace and ornate topiary of the Petwood Hotel, commandeered as No. 617 Squadron's Officers' Mess.
All photos from the author's collection.

Captains posted to the squadron usually brought their established crew with them. They were a team and their efficiency and effectiveness depended on each other. Reid was additionally unusual in that he was posted in alone without a crew. However, a week later, and by dint of a little string pulling, he was joined from No. 61 Squadron by Sergeant Les Rolton, his 21-year-old bomb aimer who he had known since his days at 29 OTU. From West Ham, after winning a scholarship to Leyton Technical College Rolton worked initially at the Plessey works in Ilford. As a schoolboy he had allegedly been told: 'You will join the RAF, shoot down 11 planes and be awarded the Victoria Cross.' After enlisting, Rolton was selected for pilot training and sent to America as part of the Arnold scheme, but any hopes of the prophecy being fulfilled were soon dispelled when he was scrubbed from his course. He remustered as an observer, but during his training the Pilot/Navigator/Bomb-aimer (PNB) scheme was introduced and Rolton emerged from this trained as a bomb aimer.

Wireless operator Flying Officer David Luker, previously of No. 29 OTU and No. 9 Squadron, had arrived at Woodhall Spa a week before. He, too, was a friend of Reid who had engineered his transfer to No. 617. Born in Gibraltar, but educated in London,

Luker was married with a wife in Sevenoaks. His mother lived less than 2 miles from Rolton's. Aged thirty, Luker enlisted in 1940 and was commissioned in 1942, being promoted to flight lieutenant in February 1943.

The rest of the crew came about as the result of tragedy. Flight Sergeant Donald 'Chunky' Stewart, the flight engineer, and the two gunners, Sergeant Holt and Warrant Officer Hutton, were already with the squadron, as part of another crew. Flight Lieutenant Tom O'Shaughnessy's aircrew had been posted to No. 617 Squadron from No. 619 on 30 September 1943. Aged twenty-five, Stewart came from South Merstham, Surrey, while the two gunners were the oldest members of the crew. Holt, thirty-one, came from Winslow, Buckinghamshire, and was married to a girl from Douglas, Isle of Man, whom he had met while training at No. 5 AOS at Jurby. Hutton, a Geordie, had just had his thirty-fourth birthday when he joined Reid's crew. Between them they had experienced action, successfully seeing off an enemy fighter outbound to Turin on 12 July 1943.

By January 1944 O'Shaughnessy and his crew had completed four operations with 617 Squadron. On the evening of 20 January he took off with a skeleton crew of four to carry out low-level practice using the

Right
Bill Reid, centre and the surviving members of his No. 61 Squadron crew. Standing: F/Sgt Les Rolton and F/Sgt Frank Emerson Seated: F/Sgt Jim Norris, Bill Reid and F/Sgt Cyril Baldwin.

spotlight altimeter (as used for the Dams Raid), when their aircraft struck the beach at Snettisham, Norfolk, killing O'Shaughnessy and his navigator, Flying Officer Arthur Holding, and badly injuring his wireless operator and bomb aimer. Hutton, Holt and Stewart attended O'Shaughnessy's funeral in Liverpool. During March they flew operations as substitutes in other crews.

The only non-British member of the crew, the navigator Flying Officer Joseph Peltier, was a French Canadian from Windsor, Ontario. Born in 1918, he had left high school after matriculation in 1936 and undertaken a one-year commercial course at Windsor Vocational School. Long-term employment was hard to come by. After working for brief periods as a clerk in a shoe store and as a sander with the Canadian Battery and Bonalite Company, he worked for three summer seasons as a farmhand before finding a permanent position in the freight shed and as a car checker with the New York Central Railroad Company. On the outbreak of war, in keeping with other men of military age, he was enlisted as a private into the Essex Scottish Regiment Non-permanent Active Militia (the Canadian Army Reserve), undertaking a month's basic military training before transferring

to the 1st Division, Royal Canadian Army Service Corps (RCASC) for a further six months.

During this period Joseph applied to transfer to the RCAF for aircrew duties, but although seen as being extremely keen he was initially rejected on account of being underweight and in poor physical condition, despite being a regular swimmer and player of hockey and basketball. After three further medicals he achieved the necessary standard and was accepted into the RCAF as an aircraftman second class, although he was initially assessed as being 'nervous and apt to become confused under tension' and was considered better suited to a ground trade such as wireless operator, rather than being promising aircrew material. By the time Peltier enlisted on 5 June 1941 his determination to fly had persuaded the authorities that he should be given a chance. After passing through No. 1 Initial Training School in Toronto it was accepted that his Link Trainer performance was too poor for him to qualify for pilot instruction and he was redirected for training as an observer. October 1941 found him posted to No. 4 Air Observers' School at Crumlin, Ontario. There he proved to be an eager pupil, with good map reading and log keeping, although overconfidence gave rise to mistakes and inaccuracy.

In the midst of his training Joseph married Lillian

Left Bill Reid and three of his No. 617 Sqn crew at Woodhall Spa, summer 1944. Left to right F/Lt Bill Reid, F/O Joseph Peltier, F/O Leslie Rolton and F/Sgt Donald Stewart.

Right After fitting its tail unit, armourers steady a Tallboy as it is lifted from the bomb dump at Woodhall Spa prior to loading onto its special bomb trolley.

Scott in Windsor, Ontario, on 17 January 1942, but there was little time for celebration, for that same day he was posted to No. 4 Bombing and Gunnery School at Fingal, flying Battles and Ansons. Qualifying on 28 February he was awarded his observer's flying badge by Wing Commander Alexander Judd Kennedy, being rated as average in both bombing and gunnery. March saw him posted to No. 2 Air Navigation School, Pennfield Ridge, New Brunswick, to complete his navigation training with an intensive four-week night navigation course. By the time he passed out it was noted that there had been a definite improvement in his performance, being seen as confident in his work, persistent and dependable.

After crossing the Atlantic in May, and the usual processing for RCAF personnel through No. 3 Personnel Reception Centre, Bournemouth, at the end of June Peltier was posted to No. 10 (Observer) Advanced Flying Unit at Dumfries to begin his acclimatisation to European topography and navigation in blackout conditions, prior to progression to No. 22 OTU at Wellesbourne Mountford in August as an

observer (B). His period at Wellesbourne was hampered by bad weather and it was not until 23 October 1942 that he was posted to No. 102 Squadron, a No. 4 Group squadron based at Pocklington, equipped with Halifax B IIs, a more complex machine than the OTU's Wellingtons. A period of conversion was required, for which he initially joined the squadron's Conversion Flight, which was being merged into No. 1652 Conversion Unit, at Marston Moor, as part of the revised PNB programme being introduced to familiarise crews with the four-engined 'heavies'. As a result of this scheme, Sergeant Peltier became recategorised from observer (B/A) to navigator (B).

Peltier returned to No. 102 Squadron on 5 January 1943 as part of Warrant Officer Alexander Younger's crew. His first three operations were 'gardening' sorties (minelaying), the first accompanied by the squadron commander, Wing Commander George Holden (who went on to command No. 617 Squadron in August 1943 and was killed in the disastrous attack on the Dortmund–Ems Canal the following month). Peltier's first venture to the Reich came on 2 February

Clockwise from left
The southern
entrance to the Rilly
la Montagne railway
tunnel; Rilly la
Montagne tunnel,
northern entrance;
A water filled Tallboy
crater in woodland
above the Rilly tun-
nel, today known as
the 'Six tonne' by
local inhabitants.

when the crew attacked Cologne. The remainder of the tour read like a gazetteer of German cities. There were single trips to Berlin, Hamburg, Essen, Munich, Kiel, Frankfurt and Stettin, two to Stuttgart and three to Duisburg. Targets further afield included Turin and the Škoda works at Pilsen. During an attack on Nuremberg on 25 February the Halifax's air-speed indicator iced up over the Thames Estuary on the outward route and remained frozen all the way to the target (which was reached within five minutes of the planned ETA, a tribute to Peltier's skill), only thawing out as they approached the French coast on the homeward leg. Three nights later, while over St-Nazaire, a loud crash was heard against the Halifax's fuselage and the flight engineer reported being hit on the arm by an object. After leaving the target a search was made and the nose of a 4-lb incendiary bomb was found in the navigator's compartment. On return to base it was found that this had caused serious damage to a former and longeron, while a strike by another bomb had damaged the starboard fin. Friendly fire again gave cause for concern on 10 April. En route to Frankfurt

the crew were fired on by the rear turret of another four-engined aircraft below and on the port bow, a single burst striking the constant-speed unit of the port inner engine and putting it out of action. Ten nights later over Stettin they were hit by light flak that caused damage to the port side near the wireless operator's position.

Whether the result of this close call, or for other reasons, Joe Peltier was deemed to have completed his first tour at the end of February 1943, having completed only twenty-four operations. Promoted to temporary warrant officer in March, he was posted as an instructor to No. 23 OTU, Pershore, on 9 May 1943. By June he had been commissioned. After a year as an instructor he learned of Reid's search for a wireless operator and put in a request, forfeiting an opportunity to return to Canada in order to join No. 617 Squadron for operational flying. This was granted and he arrived at Woodhall Spa on 3 March 1944.

By April, Reid and his newly assembled crew had completed sufficient training to establish the

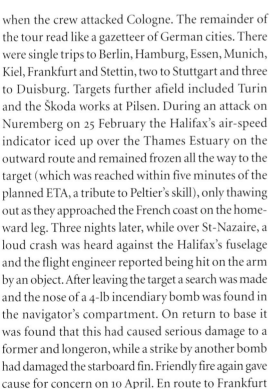

Right W/Cdr John Bell (left), bomb aimer with F/O Bob Knights' crew on 31 July 1944, and the author at the dedication of the Rilly La Montagne memorial, June 2009.

teamwork and coordination essential to commence operations. Their first two trips were to the Paris marshalling yards of Juvisy and La Chapelle on 18 and 19 April, where No. 617 were marking the target for the remainder of No. 5 Group. The next two sorties initiated the squadron's marking technique against German targets with attacks on Brunswick and Munich. As a relatively new crew, they were used to back up the initial marking by the squadron with incendiaries and high explosives.

Following Munich the squadron was sent on leave. On their return they found themselves screened from operations while they developed and perfected the specialist 'Window'-dropping technique for Operation 'Taxable', the D-Day deception operation, to create the impression of an invasion fleet approaching the French coast. Although the principle had been devised by the Telecommunications Research Establishment, much work and fine-tuning was undertaken by the squadron to turn theory into operational practice. A great workload fell upon the 'navigators' union' – a fact recognised by fellow Canadian, Squadron Leader Danny Walker, the Squadron Navigation Leader who noted that Peltier 'showed outstanding interest in the development of special operational navigation'. For 'Taxable' itself, the crew carried in addition Flight Lieutenant Terry Kearns and members of his crew to assist in the flying, navigation and dispatch of 'Window'.

Three nights later, Reid and his crew were part of the force dropping the first of Barnes Wallis's 'Tallboys'

on the Saumur railway tunnel. On 14 June they participated in the attack on the E-boat pens at Le Havre, and the following day set out to inflict similar damage on the pens at Boulogne, but were thwarted by poor visibility and returned with their 'Tallboy' intact. There then followed a series of six strikes against the large V-weapon sites at Watten, Wizernes, Mimoyecques and Siracourt. The crew were on leave between 4 and 12 July, thereby missing the squadron's first attack against a V1 storage depot, that at Saint-Leu-d'Esserent; nor did they participate in the two sorties against Wizernes on 17 and 20 July, or that against Watten on the 25th. However, they knew that they must soon appear again on the battle order. Thus their inclusion would have come as no surprise when they studied the flying programme for 31 July and found their names listed for an assault on the storage depot in the tunnel at Rilly-la-Montagne.

Throughout the previous two months, 'Tallboy's' unique capability meant that the squadron had operated generally as a single unit. On a few occasions when they worked in conjunction with other squadrons from No. 5 Group (such as those against Le Havre and Boulogne), they was given separate aiming points and bombed before the rest of main force to ensure clear visibility, unhindered by smoke and dust from other bombing. The unqualified success of 'Tallboy' on its first use, against the railway tunnel at Saumur, would make it logical to dispatch the squadron alone to deal with this target. Yet its importance was such that a force of at least ninety-seven Lancasters from four bases within No. 5 Group was to be sent to bomb both the north and south tunnel entrances. Some 50% of the main force aircraft would carry 1,000-pounders fused for half an hour or an hour's delay, and 10% of the others would be fused with delays ranging from 6 to 144 hours, which would serve to hinder immediate recovery work. The remaining bomb loads would detonate on impact.

No. 617 Squadron was to provide sixteen Lancasters, each carrying 'Tallboys' fused for half an hour's delay, together with two Mosquitoes for marking purposes. A point midway between the two entrances was to be marked by a No. 109 Squadron Mosquito using Oboe, providing a datum, after which No. 617 Squadron's Mosquitoes would carry out precision marking of each of the tunnel entrances. The squadron would then attack first, bombing from around 16,000 feet, following which the main force would come in and bomb from 18,000 feet. The height differential was essential, along with precise timing, to ensure a clear target for No. 617's aircraft and enable them to clear the area prior to the main force attack. On hearing this at briefing, a number of No. 617 crews expressed concern, as there was little margin for error if things did not go exactly to plan. However, no changes were made.

Reid and his crew were ninth to take off, at 17.51

hours. Seven minutes later all sixteen aircraft were airborne and course was set for Reading, thence out over Selsey Bill, turning mid-Channel towards the French coast at Le Tréport. There they met their Spitfire escort in a clear blue sky. Spasmodic flak was encountered as they headed across France, but nothing to cause concern. Reid had taken his camera with him, and shot a few photographs of other aircraft in the formation. At first all appeared to be going according to plan. However, the strength of a briefed tailwind had been underestimated, making it increasingly difficult to adhere to the predetermined speeds and timings. No. 83 Squadron aircraft – their fins marked with a white vertical stripe and firing green Very lights to identify themselves as leading the main force behind No. 617 – frequently found themselves being overtaken by following aircraft, forcing the pace.

In consequence, No. 83 Squadron arrived over the target at 20.17 hours, two minutes ahead of their scheduled time. The weather was good and since the target could be clearly identified the main force leader gave the order to bomb. As a result, the first bombs were already falling by the time the Oboe markers went down a minute later. This failure to adhere to timings now compromised the whole operational plan and jeopardised the safety of the 'Tallboy' force.

A moderate barrage of heavy flak opened up over the target shortly after bombing commenced. Reid saw the tell-tale bursts ahead. The confused timings meant that the squadron's specific aiming points had not been marked; however, they could be easily recognised and the bombing run was completed without incident. Reid felt the aircraft lift as the 'Tallboy' fell away. Holding the Lancaster straight and level he mentally counted the seconds necessary to secure his aiming point photograph. Suddenly the aircraft gave a violent lurch, followed by a second, more forceful reaction. Reid struggled to comprehend the significance. The Lancaster had been hit by two 1,000-pounders from a main force aircraft, one striking the port mainplane, the other the fuselage between the cockpit and mid-upper turret. Reid quickly assessed the situation, calling: 'Stand by to bale out.' The port outer engine had broken away, and with the control runs severed the control column was slack and useless. Realising the situation was hopeless he ordered the crew to abandon aircraft.

'Chunky' Stewart handed Reid his chest-style para-

Left The Rilly La Montagne memorial with a wreath laid on behalf of the No. 617 Squadron Association, June 2009.

Right A pressure bottle salvaged from the wreckage of ME557 KC-S and converted into a drinking flask.

Below Presentation of the bottle to No. 617 Squadron at the Petwood Hotel, November 2009. Left to-right: S/Ldr Tony Griffiths, F/Lt Lucy Williams, F/Lt Edward Dudley and F/Lt Alex Hutchison.

chute and moved down into the nose, followed by Peltier. The redistribution of weight caused the aircraft to enter a steepening dive, throwing Reid forward, preventing him from leaving his seat. He pulled off his helmet and tried without success to open the side window. Remembering the ditching exit in the canopy roof, he reached upwards and turned the release handle clockwise. As he did so, the entire nose section of the aircraft disintegrated and he fell clear. There was a whirring sound in his ears, then everything went quiet and he was falling through space. He managed to pull the D-ring on his parachute. After what seemed an inordinate amount of time – causing him to think that the 'chute had not worked – there was an explosion above him, followed by a jerk. He looked up and saw the canopy deployed above him. Fearful that his parachute pack was not clipped on properly he held the shroud lines tightly. His right hand was numb, having struck the aircraft as he was sucked out and he was unable to control his descent. Another worrying thought then struck him: he might get hit by pieces of aircraft as he descended. On further reflection he realised that most of it would already be below him.

Reid saw trees approaching; aware that he could do nothing to avoid them he kept his legs together hoping to prevent any serious damage. One leg went dead as he struck a treetop; he thought it might be broken. Divesting himself of his harness and parachute he slid painfully down the trunk, a task made even more difficult by his injured hand. On reaching the ground he found that he could still stand and walk. Conscious that his face was bleeding he applied a field dressing to the wound, after which his thoughts turned to evasion. He buried his Mae West and checked his escape kit. He still had his revolver, issued to aircrew shortly before D-Day, but his ammunition pouch was empty. Without ammunition the revolver was useless; he disposed of it in some bushes.

While taking stock of his situation he heard the delayed-action bombs beginning to detonate. Paris was some 30 miles away. His French was passable so there was a chance that he might be able to evade capture and make contact with friendly locals who would be able to assist him to the Allied lines. He set off, heading south, using the compass from his escape kit. About half an hour later, after travelling a mile or so, he stopped to consult his escape map. Looking up suddenly, he saw three German troops approaching with rifles and fixed bayonets. They challenged him, at first thinking he was American because it was a daylight attack. Injured, in uniform and outnumbered, there was no option but to surrender.

After making sure Reid was unarmed and capable of walking the soldiers led him back along the edge of a wood. Spotting a piece of the tail section of a Lancaster protruding from the trees he pointed to it and asked if he could go and look at it. It was part of his aircraft. The rear turret had broken off and come to rest about 20 yards away, with John Hutton still inside. The body of Bert Holt was discovered inside the rear fuselage, slumped by the rear entrance door. His parachute was attached to him, but he'd had no time to jump. The front section of the aircraft was nowhere to be seen. Reid was hopeful that the rest of the crew had been able to bale out. If so, they stood a good chance of evading capture. He was sure that Peltier, being French Canadian would be OK and Stewart was a strong reliable type, well able to look after himself.

Twenty minutes later they came upon another group of soldiers escorting another prisoner. It was David Luker, his wireless operator. Luker's parachute had opened inside the aircraft and was torn, resulting in a faster than desirable descent. He had landed heavily, twisting his ankle and knocking himself out. He came round to find an armed German standing over him. Reid and Luker were taken to a nearby flak battery, where a doctor tended their injuries, after which they followed the usual route into captivity, via Dulag Luft, Oberursel, arriving at Stalag Luft III, Sagan, on 12 August. Reid was subsequently transferred to Stalag Luft III, Belaria, a separate camp 5 kilometres from Sagan. At the end of January 1945 Luker and Reid were among those forced to evacuate their camps and march west, away from the advancing Soviet forces. They arrived at Stalag Luft IIIA, Luckenwalde, on 6 February and remained there until the Soviets arrived on 22 April. Even so, their ordeal was not over and it was not until 20 May that the Russians took them to the Elbe, where they were handed over to the Americans. From there they were flown to Brussels, to await a further repatriation flight to the UK. Reid arrived back at RAF Cosford on 27 May 1945. Leaving the RAF in November 1945 Reid obtained a BSc in agriculture and became an adviser to Spillers. In

retirement he was an active member of many organisations, becoming vice president of the Aircrew Association. He died in November 2001. David Luker remained in the RAF until March 1958. He moved to South Africa and died in the 1980s.

The loss of Reid's aircraft was witnessed by a number of crews: Flying Officer Jupp of No. 83 Squadron recorded: 'One Lancaster was seen to go down near the target at 2021 hrs. Three [sic] parachutes were seen to open. The dinghy also fell out and fell down with the tailplanes and rear turret.' Several of No. 49 Squadron crews reported spotting a Lancaster in trouble over the target. It was on fire and broke in two as it fell to the ground; parachutes were observed. Flying Officer Squibb of the same squadron, however, offered a different interpretation: 'Lancaster suspected hit by bomb from aircraft above as no flak seen.'

Most telling perhaps is the report for Flying Officer Archer of No. 106 Squadron: 'One bomb seen to hit Lancaster flying just beneath but the Lancaster continued on its way.' This refers to only one bomb and the indication is that the lower aircraft survived. The wording is also open to interpretation. Is this merely an observation by a neighbouring aircraft, or was the bomb part of Archer's own load? Was the lower aircraft Reid's or another that Lady Luck chose to disregard that evening?

The official overall assessment of the operation compiled from an analysis of all crew reports recorded: 'At Rilly la Montagne fairly heavy predicted flak was experienced at 16,000–17,000 feet ... [a] Lancaster was seen to blow up, hit by falling bombs from another aircraft. 4 parachutes were seen to open.'

Among another of No. 617 Squadron's crews, captain Lieutenant Nick Knilans, an American serving in Bomber Command, recorded a narrow escape that day in his memoirs. Early on the bombing run his flight engineer, Flying Officer Ken Ryall, tapped him urgently on the shoulder, telling him to look up. About a hundred feet directly above was another squadron aircraft, with bomb doors open. Knilans kicked the rudder and skilfully jinked his Lancaster to one side into clear air. A few minutes later the implications were brought home when his rear gunner reported seeing another of the squadron's aircraft being hit by a bomb and breaking up. Two parachutes were observed before it hit the ground.

No. 617 Squadron were not the only ones at risk.

Right F/Sgt Holt's
headstone, Paris City
Cemetery, Clichy.

Below W/O John
Hutton's grave,
Paris City Cemetery,
Clichy.

Flying Officer Foot of No. 83 Squadron, bombing
from 18,000 feet at the same time as No. 617 Squadron
made their run, reported: 'No difficulty in managing
bombing run but sharp look out necessary for bombs
from other aircraft above. One 12,000lb bomb fell
just 200 yards past my starboard wing.' If these details
are correct, they indicate that at least one of No. 617's
crews was sufficiently concerned to ignore their briefed
slot and bomb from a greater height. If so, there is
(perhaps not surprisingly) no record of any such
deviation in the squadron records.

Despite these accounts, the identity of the aircraft
struck by bombs could not be immediately confirmed.
The squadron's official notification of the loss of
Reid's aircraft to the Air Ministry states: 'There were
some 200 aircraft over the target at one time, therefore it was not possible for other crew of this Squadron to confirm the circumstances in which this
aircraft became a casualty. The aircraft has therefore
been classified Missing, as nothing was heard from it
after take off.'

Writing to next of kin, Wing Commander Tait
informed them: 'The aircraft failed to return to base
and very little is known of the circumstances in which
it failed to return. There were many aircraft over the
target at the same time, and the only information I
have is from returning crews, who reported seeing
some personnel abandon an aircraft by parachute.
You will appreciate that at such a time it is difficult
to formulate a conclusion clearly, but I think that
there is a strong possibility that your husband may
have landed safely.' There now followed the inevitable,
agonising, wait for news.

For Reid's mother, at home in Ballieston, Glasgow,
that news arrived on 24 September when she received
the simple message: 'Don't be worried about me as I
am all right and in good health.'

However, five other families faced the gradually
emerging reality that a son, husband or brother would
not be returning home.

The Germans soon located the remains of the nose
of Reid's Lancaster, further to the east than the tail
section. Inside the wreckage they found the bodies of
Les Rolton and Joseph Peltier. They and the two gunners were buried in the West Cemetery in Reims on
2 August. The body of Donald Stewart was only found
a week after his death, having been thrown out of the

Lancaster as it broke up. He was buried separately on 8 August, alone and initially unidentified, in the parish cemetery at Germaine, 2 miles south of his target. The confirmation of these casualties took time to filter through from German notification to the International Red Cross, then to the Air Ministry Casualty Branch who would tell the next of kin. Information was not always complete or conclusive and had to be checked. Having received the initial communication that her husband was missing, Joe Peltier's wife was advised that this meant that his aircraft had failed to return and that his whereabouts were unknown, but that he might be a prisoner of war. His name would not appear in official casualty lists for five weeks. But by the end of October 1944 news had been received from German sources that Joe Peltier was dead. His family were informed, but until further details were available he was to be reclassified as 'Missing, believed killed in action.' It was to be another year until it was asserted that 'Flying Officer Joseph Peltier is now for official purposes presumed to have died on Active Service Overseas on July 31 1944.'

The difficulties of absorbing this news were compounded when information was received in September 1944 that the bodies of Rolton, Hutton, Holt and, it was later confirmed, Peltier, had been transferred from Reims to the newly established temporary American Cemetery at Champigneul. By June 1945 they had again been moved, this time to their final resting place: Rolton, Hutton and Holt to the cemetery at Clichy, in the northern suburbs of Paris, and Peltier to the Canadian Cemetery at Hautot-sur-Mer, near Dieppe.

In August 2006, veterans and families of Canadians who died during the ill-fated 1942 Operation 'Jubilee' Allied raid on Dieppe, paid a visit to the French coastal town. Their pilgrimage visited the cemetery containing the graves of 761 servicemen, including 75 members of the Essex Scottish Regiment, the unit that had provided Peltier with his basic military training. Among those attending was Joe Peltier's widow, Lillian, whose younger brother had been wounded and taken prisoner at Dieppe. After paying her respects at her husband's grave she expressed appreciation that he had been finally laid to rest among 'the home boys' – all the friends he knew and with whom he went to school. ◉

Left F/O Leslie Rolton's headstone, Paris City Cemetery, Clichy.

Below The grave of Reid's Flight Engineer, F/Sgt Donald Stewart, Germaine Communal Cemetery, two miles south of the tunnel.

CHAPTER NINE

YOU DID YOUR DUTY...
MY BROTHERS IN ARMS

BY MARC HALL

HALIFAX LW436 OF NO. 434 SQUADRON, BASED AT RAF CROFT, SOUTH OF DARLINGTON, WAS DETAILED FOR A SORTIE LATE MORNING ON 4 AUGUST 1944 TO ATTACK THE SUPPLY DUMP AT BOIS DE CASSAN, BELIEVED TO BE STORING V1 FLYING BOMBS. THE SITE, INSIDE DENSE WOODLAND, CONSISTED OF NUMEROUS BUNKERS AND STORAGE FACILITIES, WITH ACCOMPANYING AIR DEFENCES. ON THIS DAY 291 AIRCRAFT OF NOS 6 AND 8 GROUPS DEPARTED THEIR BASES TO ATTACK BOIS DE CASSAN AND ALSO THE TROSSY ST MAXIMIN SITE. THE WEATHER WAS CLEAR OVER THE TARGET AREAS AND THE RAIDS WERE SUCCESSFULLY CARRIED OUT, WITH THE LOSS OF ONLY FOUR BOMBER COMMAND AIR-CRAFT. THE CREW OF HALIFAX LW436 HAD ROARED INTO THE SKY AT 10.29 HOURS THAT MORNING, FATED NEVER TO RETURN HOME.

WITH THE AIRCRAFT and crew long overdue, enquires were made to see if the Halifax had landed elsewhere. The next day, however, telegrams were sent out to the next of kin advising them that their relatives were missing in action. This was all the news they would receive until the end of September 1944, when further details became available and the Red Cross informed the families that four of the crew had indeed lost their lives, although nothing further was heard regarding the remaining three airmen. After the war a tale of struggle and survival would emerge.

Following the end of hostilities, the Missing Research and Enquiry Service (MRES) set about locating and laying to rest the fallen airmen who had not come home. It transpired the three unaccounted for aircrew of this Halifax were now known to be safe and well, and it fell to a Squadron Leader Wood and his team from the No. 6 Section of the MRES to locate the four other airmen, investigate the crash and undertake the grim task of exhumation. The team visited the small village of Drosay, a quiet farming community situated in the area of Pays de Caux, some 25 miles south-west of Dieppe, and the graves were located in the parish cemetery. The secretary of the church at Drosay, Mons Herbert, alongside statements from the survivors, supported the fact that the aircraft had exploded over the area after being hit by flak. Three of the bodies had been named from their personal identification discs, and the fourth, Sergeant Raymond Bruegeman, by a process of elimination. (The Red Cross had advised the Allies via a telegram, quoting German information, that Flying Officer J.H. Kelly and Flying Officer George Perkins, along with one non-RCAF airman and one unknown, had indeed lost their lives on the afternoon of 4 August 1944.) A number of French locals had recovered the deceased and buried them side by side with crosses made from pieces of the crashed aircraft. The graves were well kept, with flowers, the local people taking pride and great care to honour the airmen. Following their identification, the Graves Registration Unit were handed the case and their deaths were recorded for official purposes, enabling the families to have some closure. Today the four young airmen rest in the same churchyard at Drosay along with six other Allied airmen not affiliated with this crew.

Left Raymond Bruegeman. *Marilee Magder and family, Mary and Rueben.*

The young crew were only on their third operational sortie when tragedy struck. Their Halifax had reached the target area and was positioned for the bombing run, flying through a thick flak barrage with sinister large puffs of black smoke from shells exploding and rocking the aircraft as it pressed on regardless. While over the target the Halifax sustained critical damage from a nearby flak burst, sending shards of hot metal into the airframe and shredding the port elevator and rudder. The pilot, Flight Lieutenant Robert Lang, later recounted that the aircraft was becoming increasingly hard to control, but the crew carried on and successfully bombed the target at 16,000 feet before making a swift exit to the north-west in the direction of the French coast. With a damaged aircraft the skipper battled with the controls to get his boys back to base. It became apparent that two bombs had failed to release from their racks and were hung up in the bomb bay. With the pilot struggling to steer the aircraft their luck was about to run out, as German anti aircraft batteries continued to hound the fleeing bombers.

Twenty miles from the coast and near Rouen, the aircraft took a direct hit in the starboard wing, which tore open the fuel tanks, the contents spilling out over the hot, running engines and igniting instantly. With fire now raging, Flight Lieutenant Lang took imme-

Right Ray Bruegeman in 1942. *Marilee Magder and family, Mary and Rueben.*

diate action and shut down the starboard outer motor, feathering the airscrew. The flight engineer activated the fire extinguisher and quickly the fire was checked, eventually extinguished, and no longer visible from the cockpit. But Halifax LW436 was in a critical state, Lang later reporting: 'Owing to very little port elevator and rudder control and only one starboard engine, I had to close the throttle on all of the remaining engines so as to keep the aircraft under control. We could not hold our altitude, so I gave the crew the order to prepare for ditching.'

The Halifax was now heading for the cold uninviting waters of the English Channel. Without warning, the aircraft exploded, breaking into a number of large parts. Four lives abruptly ended. The remaining three survivors who had their parachutes suddenly found themselves in mid-air, but all of them landed safely. Flight Lieutenant Lang continues his story in a statement given following his return home to the UK: 'Then the fuel tank exploded and the next thing I knew I was out of the aircraft and had pulled the rip-cord on my parachute. All of this happened at 13.30 in the afternoon. I was picked up by Dr and Madam Aureille at Cany-Barville, Seine Inferieur [sic], France, a mile from the crash. The bodies of four

of the crew were found near the crash. Flying Officer George G. Perkins, Flying Officer J.H. Kelly, Pilot Officer R.G. Bruegeman, all from Ontario and Sergeant N. Marley from England. They were buried in the church yard of Drosay, Seine Inferieur, a mile from the crash site.' The two other survivors landed close together and met up, crawling into a ditch. After two days they began to look for food before finally being taken in and given shelter, subsequently returning to England.

Some letters and accounts survive, giving further detail of the tragic loss of the aircraft. The first is from Madam Eva Aureille, written to the Bruegeman family:

28 October 1946
Dear Madam:
I received your letter this morning and with the sincere hope of easing your mind and making you a little happier I am answering you by air-mail.

It was about half-past one in the afternoon of the 4 of August 1944, that a Halifax plane exploded and crashed near Drosay a few miles away from Cany where I live. I was absent at the moment but on my return at six o'clock and hearing about the accident, I went immediately to the place to see if we could do anything and help escape any of the boys if there were any still living, but all we found was the wrecked plane and a newly dug grave beside it. We searched until dark and began again the next morning at four o'clock as soon as day broke and this time we were fortunate enough to find the pilot Robert Lang severely bruised all over and hiding in a wheat field and it was through having been given the description of the body found beside the plane that we knew it was Raymond Bruegeman. The explosion was so sudden that he was thrown out of the plane without having the time to open out his parachute, he was killed instantly and was not even disfigured, so please let your mind rest at ease, everything happened so quickly that it was already over before he knew even that they were in danger. Two days later he was taken from his temporary grave, put into a very nice coffin, and was buried this time in the cemetery beside the church at Drosay after a very touching burial service. The next day the bodies of the other three poor boys were found and were also buried in the same cemetery beside your son, they had all been killed

Left Ray Bruegeman.
in 1943. *Marilee Magder
and family, Mary and
Rueben.*

immediately. Robert Lang explained to us that coming back from the target near Paris, they were crossing Rouen when the flak made a small hole in their right wing, the hole must have got bigger and bigger and at last broke off (it was found about 3 miles from the plane) at the same moment the plane exploded into 5 or 6 pieces. Robert said that they were all so far from thinking that something could happen that some of them had not even put on their parachutes. That Robert Lang has not written to you or been to see you, does not astonish me in the least. We are very disappointed in him for we risked our lives to help him and hid him a month in our house with the Germans coming in and out every day until we were liberated, and yet not one simple word of thanks have we received from him. He left us in September 1944 and was flown back to England and when I went to England myself in April 1945, I moved heaven and earth to find out what had happened to him since the commanding officer had come to our house to fetch him, at last found him and learnt that he had even been home to Canada on leave and had come back again, it was then that I gave him the photos, he promised me faithfully then to write a letter to my husband, who as you can

imagine was not very pleased with him, but we are still waiting for the letter and will probably wait a long time. Of the twelve air men I helped to escape he is the only one who has shown such rank ingratitude. Yesterday a Mrs. Michel-Taboulet came to see me saying that you had written her, asking news of your son. I gave her some photos of the church and the other boys' graves to send you, I hope you receive them safely. I again assure you Madam that your son died instantly and without even being disfigured that he was buried like a Christian and his grave is always well kept. Perhaps one day you will come and visit it yourself.

You have suffered terribly also by the war and my heartfelt sympathies goes with you and will you please give my deepest sympathy to your daughter and daughter-in-law.

My sincere best wishes to you all.
Eva Aureille

On 20 November 1946 a relative of Flying Officer Kelly wrote to Mrs Bruegeman. 'Bud' was the nickname for the pilot:

Bud was fortunate that he came down near the French couple of whom you speak, and of whom we

Right Jack Kelly. *National archives of Canada* **George Perkins.** *434 Squadron Association.*

all got snaps. He tells us his French is anything but good but she was an English lady married to this Frenchman who was probably actively connected with the French underground. At any rate, they hid Bud for several weeks. He tells me the Germans followed the usual procedure of going out to examine the plane and take anything valuable from it and from the bodies of our boys, and any who were alive would be brought out of the wreck as prisoners. That is why Bud, also the lad from the Maritimes, seemed so sure none of the boys in the plane when it reached the ground, were still alive. The Maritimes boy said in his letter, that the blast from the explosion was so terrific the boys would not survive it, and Bud said if they had been alive, even though hurt, the Germans would have lined them up. He also assured me the bodies were not burned at all, the boys died in the air as a result of the explosion before ever they hit the earth. After the Germans have looked over the wreck thoroughly, they tell the French people – bury them or do what you like with them, we don't care. The French people are very good and the boys were all buried from the little church nearby. Bud was not permitted to attend, as this would have been very foolish, even in rough working clothes the Germans

would have noticed a young man around who was not familiar to them and would have asked questions, so he was hidden in a barn a short way down the road, from which he could see the funeral procession. All the time he was there, which must have been several weeks, the French people from nearby kept fresh flowers on the graves of the boys, every day. Bud said he had only a little French money on him and when he was finally able to leave, he offered it to the lady, and she refused to even touch it, saying they were only too glad to be of any service. So he left it with her to buy flowers for the grave, or to repay in some small way the poor people who had been so faithful in taking care of the boys' graves. Immediately on his return to England, he made his report to the proper authorities, telling of the boys being buried and that he saw the funeral service, etc.

A French law student, Madam Evelyne Michel, whose father was the local mayor of the village during the German occupation, contacted the Bruegeman family after the war with further information of what occurred to their son's aircraft and crew mates. She informed them that the priest located Raymond Bruegeman in a cornfield, close to parts of the aircraft,

Left Norman Marley.
Marilee Magder
Gerald Donovan.
*Marilee Magder,
Jessica Donovan,
Ronald Perkins,
Carl Duivenvoorden
and family.*

the priest mentioning the wreckage having broken into five or six parts, with a wing being found 3 miles from the main crash site. Madam Michel said:

When we found Raymond we buried him the same day at the place he was lying, but two days later we put him in a beautiful coffin and buried him in the church cemetery at Drosay. We had splendid obsequies; all the men of the village who had fought in the 1914–1918 war were present with all the French and Allied flags, and all the people of the village and surrounding country. … Raymond's grave was covered with flowers, several people gave me money for me saying masses for him. The day after his funeral we found two other Canadians and one English lad. They were buried in the cemetery too. We did everything we could for them, but their obsequies were not quite like Raymond's.

The wireless operator, Sergeant Gerald Donovan, had his own tale to tell and spent many weeks on the run from the Germans and in hiding before finally being liberated by the advancing Canadian Army. A letter describes how he became a crew member, and relates their last sortie. Then a short story, which was published a number of years after the war, details his escapades with the rear gunner.

October 22, 1945
Dear Mrs. Bruegeman,
This is the first time I have had a chance to write you, and I am afraid I am not much of a letter writer. It sure is good that the wars are over but you poor people can never forget Ray, nor shall I, those four very fine boys that were killed in our aircraft. I first met Ray in the later part of April at OTU (operational training unit). He came to our billets one evening asking for a wireless operator for a crew, I don't know how it happened but I was the first to speak to him and so from then on we were the very best of pals. We had plenty of work to do and plenty to learn, but all the boys were anxious to make a success of it.

The later part of June we had two weeks leave, and Ray and I spent it together in London and Edinburgh, and a very enjoyable time we had. Then came Conversion Unit, now we started to fly in the Halifax and there was plenty more to learn but it only lasted

a month, and we were ready for the squadron. It was the Bluenose squadron and again we were flying in the Halifax. We had made two very successful trips both over France and we were more or less a little more confident in ourselves and each other since we had actually flown over enemy territory and had more idea of what it was like. Then when our third trip came along we listened very closely and wanted to make sure there were no mistakes. Equipment etc. was checked and rechecked as before. We reached our target, dropped the bombs, or at least Ray did, and were on our way home again. Everything was going fine when we were hit in the wing, the most vital spot, by enemy ground defences. Fire started immediately and we did what we could to put it out and it did seem to be out when there was a terrible explosion.

Just what happened after that I do not know too much about, however I do remember putting on my chute and the next thing I was on my way down. I have no idea how I left the aircraft. Finally I reached the ground not far from our rear gunner, so we were together from there on and he didn't know any more than I did except that the aircraft had broken in two and he had managed to get out of the rear part. We hid in a ditch very near to us for two days; at the end of that time we asked a French farmer for food and also where we were. Starting the second night we walked in a southerly direction getting bread and cider from the good French people when we could, until the eighth night when the farmer we went to for food was with the underground and he hid us away in his barn until more of the underground came with civilian clothes, false passports etc. and took us away in a wagon to a place where we were to stay until the Allied army came along. At our last place at Caudebec en Caux we had the very best of everything except we had to stay upstairs in the house and run to the attic if the Germans came around, which they did many times. However, the army came along and we knew we were free and safe.

It was about six weeks later that we met Lang in England and he told us that the other four boys had been killed. I do not believe that he even knew what happened to them, if they were hurled out without their chutes or just what may have happened. But if anybody knows it would be him because I am sure I do not know. Ray's position in the Halifax was quite well up in the nose of the ship, the navigator Kelly was very near. They worked at the same little table. I was next and the pilot Lang was directly over me, in all we were not over six feet apart. I was about seven or eight feet from the very front end.

I do remember Ray speak about some English friends of his and I believe at least one of them was killed or missing before we were reported missing. As for crew pictures, we did have some taken but they were at a studio being developed but I do not know where. Lang said he was going to try to find them if he could but I have not heard from him since March. I do hope that Ray's wife can carry on with the Business course, it will help her a lot to brave it off, Ray used to speak of her so often that I almost think I know her. Mrs Bruegeman, if there if anything else I can tell you I would be glad to do so but I believe I have answered at least the questions you asked.

So long for now and my God bless you all.
Gerald Donovan,
Canterbury, New Brunswick.

The following recollections are provided by Gerald Donovan, written after the war and in the third person:

They were flying above the clouds, great cumulus billowing puffs which blotted out all the view of the ground, but occasionally there was a glimpse of Paris out to the left. It was not long after they had left the target approximately 10,000 feet or so above some dense cloud when Gerald felt a heavy jar through the aircraft, which was in fact the impact of parts of an anti-aircraft shell through the starboard wing outer engine which had exploded nearby to the aircraft. Pieces of flak caused the fire in the motor and the extinguishers were activated, which appeared to have the effect of putting out the fire. Gerald informed the skipper that the aircraft was on fire and he replied: 'If the fire is out, we'll try to make it home.' They were over the French coast just then and there was only the English Channel to cross. As Gerald watched, the fire flared up again, and he shouted: 'Skipper, the whole right wing is on fire.' In reply, the pilot spoke into the bomber's intercom. 'Prepare to ditch,' he said. Enemy radar got them just when they believed that they were safe. Almost immediately after the fire flared up again the second time, there was a terrific explosion as if the gas tanks out in the wing had exploded. The right wing blew right off ripping a big hole

in the side of the bomber right near Gerald's position. He grabbed his parachute just as the plane broke in two. Actually, Gerald believed that the bomber broke into three pieces because he just caught a glimpse of the tail breaking away with the tail gunner still in it. He was flying away all by himself, but Gerald noticed that the tail gunner was cranking the machine gun blister around to get his parachute. Later he told Gerald that he just grabbed his chute and fell out. While still struggling with his own parachute, Gerald fell through that big hole in the side of the bomber. As he was falling the pilot gave him a good solid kick in the forehead above his eye. He only got one snap fastened and kept struggling to fasten the other snap hook and so there he was hanging horizontally on one hook. Looking up he saw that his parachute was just barely hooked on the support bar above him, and he prayed that it would hold. Although now free of the doomed bomber he was now in grave danger of dropping free from the parachute and risked falling to earth without it. Then he reached up, fearing that his parachute would break free of the bar securing it to his body, and pulled the rip cord. It had to be done. The chute opened with a snap and his loose-fitting boots flew off, but the fastening on the bar held. Looking down towards the ground he was drifting towards the uninviting waters of the English Channel; however, as he became lower he noticed ploughed fields and fortunately landed sideways in one of these, shoulder and head first due to the way he was suspended in the harness. A sudden and sharp pain convinced him he had broken some ribs but there was no medical aid to hand.

As he gathered up his parachute, he saw another member of the bomber crew land over in a field some distance away. That fellow immediately fell down and couldn't get up so Gerald knew that the other airman was hurt. He kept looking around for more of the crew, and at the same time wary of the presence of Germans. It was then he spotted one of their fellows running towards him and immediately recognised him as the tail gunner and, with a river of adrenalin flowing, the tail gunner took both parachutes over and hid them in the scrub. They both moved into the bushes and took stock of the situation and what they had, which was a small emergency ration and some survival equipment. All day they hid in those bushes and eventually they saw some Frenchmen attend the area and go over to the third airmen they had seen approximately four hundred yards away who was struggling to move or get up. The

Frenchmen came back for him later on and removed him to a hiding place.

Every hour the soreness in Gerald's head and chest increased. After dark they began to walk westwards as they had been taught in training. They walked all night, staying off the roads to avoid the Germans who were always moving. It was very rough on his feet without shoes as he had lost his flying boots when the parachute had snapped open. They hid in the bushes all of the following day and walked all of the next night. The tail gunner with him was very nervous and jumpy as he kept remembering flying all alone in that gun blister after the tail broke off. The two flyers had life jackets on under their parachute harness and on the third morning, they took all of that stuff off, and buried it. Gerald found out that he had quite a bad cut over his right eye and it was very sore and as such felt that he was in bad shape.

The next night as they hid they noticed several French people coming near to them and their actions told the two Canadians that the Frenchmen knew that they were there. After dark one of the Frenchmen went over to them and explained that he wanted to get them into civilian clothes as quickly as possible. Gerald told him that he needed boots. After a while, he brought a pair of boots over, but they were too small. The next day they hid in a straw stack out in the field, but some young children came to play around the stack. They were afraid that the attention would draw notice to them so they decided to move on in order to get away from the children's activity. The day after this the pair took up their hiding positions among some stacked corn stocks out in a field but a farmer then came over and hauled most of the corn stocks away. Upon his return he parted the stocks and saw the two Canadians but immediately covered them back up again and left. In the daylight he again returned but stayed well away from the two airmen as being caught with them by the Germans who were everywhere would likely end up with them all being shot. The following day another man returned to their place of hiding and removed them to a barn where he then questioned them and informed them that the French underground wanted to speak to them.

On the eighth day after they were shot down, a civilian came to them and he could speak perfect English. He questioned them to find out who they actually were, giving them a long examination, all about Canada. He asked Gerald dozens of details about New Brunswick

where he came from, then he asked the tail gunner all about Alberta where he came from. Questions were asked all about the rivers, the industry, the farming, many of the local places, and he knew all of the answers. After a while he seemed satisfied that they were who they said [they] were.

Then they were taken to another house where they were put up on the third floor in what was believed [to be] the attic. Although the French people had barely enough to eat themselves, they were able to find food for the two Canadians. At night they could go out into the fields and walk around. Up in their part of the attic hidden behind the bricks of a fireplace was a radio which they used to listen to, especially the BBC newscast about the war. It was from this they found out the Allied developments and the progress of the war.

Later, the men came to the two Canadians and invited them to attend a sabotage patrol with them. They went along walking up the road, five or six abreast, all ages, with some as young as sixteen and seventeen. There must have been about seventy-five of them all together. Gerald and his buddy did not speak French and so had no idea what they were supposed to do or where they were going. In fact he believed that they were just in the way. They shot up a bridge that night, but Gerald didn't know what damage was done. On another day, the two flyers watched as Allied fighter bombers attacked a nearby bridge with a number of Mosquito planes destroying it.

A visit was made to the mayor's house where everything was spoken in English but, nevertheless, not knowing what was going on, they were always nervous, and being tense and ready to run all of the time was very tiring. The village where the mayor resided was on the bank of a river and they soon discovered it had some secrets. The Canadian army had advanced and they were on the bank on the other side of the river, meaning rescue was now so near. The French told Gerald that they should cross the river to the Canadians. At first Gerald didn't even know that the Canadians were there and of course they didn't trust anyone at any time. It was then they learned that the village was also hiding about a dozen other Allied personnel, most of whom were Americans and they had been right in the village all of the time, but their presence was of course kept secret all of the time. Two of them took a canoe and paddled over to the Canadian army where they were met by an armed soldier from a Highland regiment. He kept his rifle aimed right on Gerald and his companion and upon crossing he challenged them in a determined manner. The prisoners were then informed to go back across the river and wait. Some of the Americans had been hiding in that village for weeks, and all were excited about getting across the river. The next day the Frenchmen

Time Carried Forward:—	202·25	128·05
Remarks (Including results of bombing, gunnery, exercises, etc.)	Flying Times
	Day	Night
OPERATIONS - ACQUET	4:35	4:35
OPERATIONS - FORET DE NIEPPE	4:30	
OPERATIONS - MISSING.		

got a boat and all of the flyers got into it and crossed over to the Canadians again and it was from there they were taken to the French coast and put on a ship bound for England. That was a happy trip. In England they were immediately sent to a centre for returned prisoners of war and they were given a medical and clothing that fit. Those needing care and treatment were tended to. The escaped flyers had arrived in old clothes and boots which were too big or too small for most of them and they were glad to throw them away. They were confined to one barrack block and there was a constant guard on the place. They were all extremely nervous and Gerald had lost fifty pounds in weight from his experience. With the guards and all, it wasn't as if they were really free, or back with friends. Of course the authorities had to find out who they really were. The military police kept them in that special barracks for about a month and all that time Gerald was most anxious to get word back to his parents to tell them that he was all right and back in England. They were told that they were confined to barracks and that there were no phones. However, one guard was sympathetic and he made it easy for Gerald to get to a phone to call home.

During his medical, Gerald's extreme nervousness showed, and it was concluded that his flying days were over and so he was declared unfit for aircrew duty. Gerald Donovan spent over a month in hiding and running and said that it was very stressful and risky most of the time. 'There never was enough food and the food was barely enough to sustain us and we all lost a lot of weight.'

A while after the war Gerald was in Moncton in a restaurant with a coupe of friends and suddenly heard a commotion. A fellow had jumped up onto a table and he came running towards them, right across the top of all of the tables. Glasses and dishes went flying. In amazement Gerald recognized his old pilot, the one who had injured his back when he landed parachuting into France. He had last seen him on the ground way out in that field. They grabbed one another, hugged and slapped each other, both talking and laughing at once. Gerald had thought that he was dead. Of course the police came and arrested both of them despite them paying for the damages but Gerald remembered that he knew the magistrate and so following a phone call and having explained everything the pair were released. It was a very happy day. Gerald settled back into civilian life as the owner and operator of a small men's clothing store. ●

CHAPTER TEN

'IT'S OUR DEREK'

BY STEVE DARLOW

AS THE NORMANDY LAND BATTLE PROGRESSED, THE ALLIED ARMIES OVERRAN THE V1 LAUNCH SITES AND THE IMMEDIATE FLYING-BOMB THREAT DIMINISHED. HOWEVER, THE MENACE OF THE V2 ROCKETS REMAINED AND IT WOULD NOT BE POSSIBLE TO DEFEND AGAINST THEM WITH FIGHTER AIRCRAFT AND ANTI-AIRCRAFT GUNS. ALLIED INTELLIGENCE STROVE TO IDENTIFY POTENTIAL TARGETS FOR ATTACK – LAUNCH SITES AND STORAGE DEPOTS. ON 31 AUGUST 1944 BOMBER COMMAND COMMENCED A CONSIDERABLE ASSAULT ON THE SITES, WITH 418 LANCASTERS, 147 HALIFAXES AND 36 MOSQUITOES DISPATCHED TO LOCATE AND BOMBARD 9 SITES IN NORTHERN FRANCE; 6 AIRCRAFT WOULD NOT BE RETURNING, WITH 27 LIVES LOST, INCLUDING THE NO. 166 SQUADRON LANCASTER OF FLIGHT ENGINEER DEREK BUTCHER.

IN 1973 BOMBER Command veteran Derek Butcher took up master engineer duties with the Royal Air Force Battle of Britain Memorial Flight. His job was to fly in the last British airworthy Lancaster and ensure that it could grace the skies at air shows and events and commemorate all the aircrew of Bomber Command who had seen active service during the Second World War. Indeed, Derek had been one of those airmen. He had flown the Lancaster into battle twenty-nine years before. Along with his crew, Derek had played his part in the Allied air offensive, including attacks on V-weapon targets, and it was on one such raid that his aircraft would be designated 'failed to return'.

Robert Derek Butcher joined the RAF in October 1942, having just turned eighteen. Following initial training at Bridlington he got to grips with flight engineering duties at RAF St Athan, and was deemed ready to progress to a Bomber Command Heavy Conversion Unit in early 1943, to assist a fledgling crew convert from experience on two-engined aircraft to the RAF's four-engined heavy bombers. Throughout March 1944 Derek flew next to his pilot, Sergeant Kernahan, on Handley Page Halifaxes at RAF Blyton and No. 1662 Conversion Unit. Scribed in Derek's logbook for 24 March, was 'Bulls Eye & Diversion Raid', a 6 hour 30 minute flight navigational exercise over enemy-occupied France trying to divert enemy attention from a large main force attack on Berlin. Derek's skills were certainly put to the test that night, with the failure of two engines, and Sergeant Kernahan fighting to maintain height. Following the transmission of an emergency 'Darkie' the crew were instructed to divert to an American airfield, their problems compounded when the runway lights were switched off. When Kernahan heard his wireless operator bark 'pull up, pull up' over the intercom – having seen the ground approaching far too quickly – Derek applied full power to the two serviceable engines and Kernahan hauled the control column back. The summit of a hill passed just beneath, although it gave up some of its tree branches, which later were removed from the Halifax's undercarriage.

Derek completed another cross-country with Sergeant Kernahan on 26 March, the last time he would fly with this pilot. There is an entry at the top of his relevant logbook page, for 1662 Conversion Unit, that states 'Unable to complete log due to loss of crew', but it has not been possible to discover the exact fate of Sergeant Kernahan.

Derek teamed up with Flying Officer Tutty, completing their first circuits and landings on 30 April, still on Halifaxes, and training continued through May. Following a spell at RAF Hemswell to learn the nuances of the Avro Lancaster, the crew arrived at RAF Kirmington and No. 166 Squadron, flying their first operational sortie on the night of 10/11 June, attacking the rail yards at Achères as part of the Transportation Plan in direct support of the Normandy invasion – an attempt to hinder the enemy's reinforcement manoeuvres.

On 22 June the crew flew a daylight raid to the V-weapon site at Mimoyecques, releasing their load over the target at 15.48 hours from 15,000 feet. A burst of heavy flak peppered the Lancaster with splinters; the port wing outboard of the port outer engine was shredded and the bomb aimer was wounded.

Left New recruit Derek Butcher, eighteen years old. *Pauline Roose.*

Left to right
Derek and friends in some kind of non-regulation activity; Derek Butcher, aged twenty one, when flying Sunderlands.
Pauline Roose.

On 23/24 June it was back to attacking rail yards, at Saintes, and the following night an attempt to knock out the V1 launch site at Flers. The next three raids were all in response to the V1 threat: a night strike on the launch site at Château Bernapré on 27/28 June; a daylight to the 'supply site' at Domléger on 29 June; and a further daylight to Oisemont/Neuville-aux-Bois the following day.

Into July and the crew's attention switched to supporting the Normandy battle, attacking rail yards on 4/5 July (Orleans), 5/6 July (Dijon) and 12/13 July (Revigny), with daylight assaults on enemy troop concentrations – trying to break the enemy's ground resistance – around Caen on 7 and 18 July, and then in the Villers-Bocage–Caumont area on 30 July. In between the crew completed their first sorties into German airspace with two night raids to Stuttgart on 24/25 and 25/26 July.

Almost a month passed before Derek 'went over the top' again, completing a long 9 hour 30 minute sortie to Stettin on 29/30 August, followed by a much shorter 2 hour 5 minute trip the next night. The exact target is not recorded in Derek's logbook – he simply states 'Ops Nr Abbeville'.

It was supposed to be similarly short raid the following night, with No. 166 Squadron's Lancasters to be part of a 601 aircraft assault upon V2 rocket sites in northern France – Flight Lieutenant Tutty's crew were designated for the attack on Agenville. In fact Tutty's Lancaster was only in the air for just over an hour before crashing to French soil not far from the target – one of six Lancasters lost on these raids (four on the Agenville attack).

Two men would lose their lives from Tutty's crew, the other five eventually returning to England. Derek and his pilot came home a few months before the war's end, at which point they were able to provide a description of the night they were shot down. (The wireless operator on the crew was Donald Pleasance, who would be captured and see out the war as a prisoner. After the conflict Donald would become an internationally renowned actor, notably starring as a prisoner-of-war in *The Great Escape* feature film). The Bomber Command Operation Research Section's 'K' report (Report of Loss of Aircraft on Operations) records Derek and Flight Lieutenant Tutty's graphic account of what happened inside their Lancaster that fateful night.

Left Youthful and eager, Derek Butcher and fellow trainees. Derek has marked his position with a pen line under his chin, 4th row up on the right. *Pauline Roose.*

Aircraft: Lancaster III, NE112 'M' of 166 Squadron
Date of Loss: 31st August 1944
Target: Agenville
Cause of Loss: Heavy flak followed by fire
Information from: Flight Lieutenant Tutty, E.B., Pilot and Captain on 18th operation. Sergeant. Butcher, R.D. Flight Engineer, on 17th operation.
Remainder of Crew: Navigator: Flying Officer Wallis. D.A. on 17th operation; Air Bomber: F/S Kirkby G.J. on 10th operation; Wireless Operator: Flying Officer Pleasance. D. on 18th operation; Mid Upper Gunner: Sergeant Letten. L. on 18th operation; Rear Gunner: Sergeant Alderson. W.C. on 19th operation

Narrative: *The squadron had to make a rushed take-off and this aircraft being the last to become airborne was not able to catch up with the rest of the force. An uneventful flight was made as far as the French coast, where the voice of the Master Bomber was heard ordering crews to descend below cloud base and bomb from a height of 9,000 feet. The Lancaster at once began to descend through cloud, which formed a solid layer at about 10,000 feet, and on breaking cloud the pilot could*

see the target ahead of him. By this time the Master Bomber had gone home and the whole force had bombed with the exception of two aircraft which could be seen about two miles ahead, near the target, heavily engaged by predicted flak. The pilot, nevertheless, decided to carry on and complete his mission, and two minutes later the bombing run was begun at a height of 9,000 feet.

As the Lancaster came within range of the target's defences, the enemy batteries opened up, 'probably of 88 mm calibre and at least six in number'. Shells burst close by and buffeted the Lancaster, and as the bomb aimer prepared to release his explosive cargo, shell fragments ripped into the port inner engine.

The Wireless Operator at once reported that the port inner engine was on fire; flames were streaming from the exhaust manifolds, and it appeared that petrol from a severed feed-pipe in the engine had come into contact with the hot exhausts, caught fire, and was continuing to feed the flames.

Derek immediately feathered the engine, 'which came to rest without difficulty' and then pressed the

Right Agenville target photograph from Flying Officer Devereau's aircraft, taken on 31 August 1944. *Sean Feast*

Graviner switch. 'The flames disappeared and seemed to be extinguished.'

The pilot continued his bombing run and the target was satisfactorily bombed. As the aircraft continued to fly straight and level on its photographic run, shells continued to burst around it. The pilot felt two severe bumps, after which the aircraft became difficult to control. Although nothing was reported by the crew, it is likely that the tail of the aircraft was struck and seriously damaged by these two bursts; since also, nothing was heard on the intercommunication system from either of the two gunners at any time after the two bumps, it is likely that the intercommunication in the rear half of the aircraft was put out of action at the same time. The aircraft showed a strong tendency to roll over to starboard onto its back, and the pilot said he had to throttle back the starboard engines and apply full port runner in order to keep it on an even keel.

With the elevator control also damaged, the Lancaster went into a shallow dive, 'in spite of the pilot's efforts with the control column and the elevator trim to keep the nose of the aircraft up'. As their height fell, Tutty ordered his crew to put on parachutes, while he tried to surmise the extent of the damage, thinking 'it was the central surfaces and not the central rods that were damaged, and that the port rudder was probably the most seriously damaged of the central surfaces'.

Shortly after, Donald Pleasance called his pilot's attention to the port wing, where the fire had spread to the No. 2 tank between the two port engines, Tutty seeing 'flames coming through the top surface of the wing all round the outline of the fuel tank'.

Since there was now no hope of saving the aircraft, the pilot gave the order to 'abandon aircraft; emergency jump', which was acknowledged by all the crew except the two gunners. The pilot next tried to reach for the emergency call-light button in order to warn the gunners, but he found that as soon as he took one hand off the control column the aircraft lurched to starboard, and he was only able to prevent the aircraft rolling onto its back by pressing on the column with both hands. He eventually had to give up trying to warn the gunners, and he suggests in the interests of the safety of other crews that the pilot's emergency call-light button in all heavy bombers should be situated on the control column and not at the side of the cockpit.

Meanwhile the crew, except for the two gunners, had collected at the front of the aircraft, and the wireless operator had fixed on the pilot's parachute. The bomb aimer spent about a minute struggling with the front escape hatch, which he was unable to open. The flight engineer then came to his assistance, opened and jettisoned the hatch, and himself baled out first. The bomb-aimer and navigator followed, and the wireless-operator, after reporting to the pilot that the mid-upper gunner had left his turret, also baled out from the front hatch.

Within seconds the Lancaster was seen to explode, Tutty remembering nothing until he woke up on the ground with his parachute open:

… it is likely that he was knocked unconscious and blown out of the aircraft by the explosion. Almost certainly the explosion took place in the burning port No. 2 petrol tank; the aircraft was at a height of about 1,500 feet at the time, and crashed immediately afterwards about 10 miles South of the target.

The pilot was captured by the enemy as he regained consciousness; he was suffering from extensive cuts and bruises, and also had one cervical vertebra and two dorsal vertebra fractured. It is likely that these injuries were caused by the explosion of the aircraft, although they may have been sustained on landing.

It was also understood that the navigator had fractured his pelvis, the bomb aimer had bruised his legs and the wireless operator was uninjured, although all three would see out the war as prisoners.

No evidence of any kind exists concerning the fate of the two missing gunners. It seems however that they were almost certainly killed in the aircraft, either by flak fragments during the original engagement or else in the final crash.

Personal notes made by Derek give further insight into the difficulties they had that night, and go on to describe his subsequent movements. In addition Derek was able to file an evasion report.

That day we had two briefings due to bad weather. We eventually took off at 13.20. On arriving over the target it was covered by cloud and icing conditions were bad. The Master Bomber kept changing his instructions, which did not help as we were being hit by accurate heavy flak on the run in. We were hit badly in the port wing and an engine was on fire. The fire extinguishers would not quell the flames. If I remember correctly we dropped the bomb load and then came the order to bale out.

I helped the bomb aimer to open the para hatch in the nose and left the aircraft. I must of [sic] blacked out as when I came to I was floating down on my chute and there was no sight of aircraft or crew. As I neared the ground I saw people running across the field I was going to land in. They were Germans and started to fire at me – as a warning I hope. On landing rather heavily, damaging my ankles and right knee slightly, the Germans

Left A series of photographs showing Derek with the Belgian families who helped with his evasion.
Pauline Roose.

had me before I was out of my parachute harness. I was surrounded and all pointing rifles at me. They searched me and took everything I had. I was taken to a farm house where an old French lady kindly bathed my feet in hot water, which was a great help.

I was then taken to a railway siding where there was a large shed which the Germans were using as an operational centre. They realised I could not speak German so left me in a corner of the shed. At that point it was difficult for me to walk without a lot of pain. I slept on the floor with other German[s]. Later that night a train arrived and I was taken on board. It was full of German soldiers.

[Derek's evasion report:] At 01.00 hrs (2 Sep) I was put on a train and arrived at 06.00 hrs at St. Pol.

[Derek's notes:] We travelled most of that night. Some soldiers shared their meals with me – raw eggs and black bread washed down with wine. Early in the morning we stopped at a railway siding and all got off. I was taken to a large house and interrogated by an army officer who spoke English. He told me I was being taken to a German POW camp.

Right The resting place of William Alderson and Lennard Letten at St. Riquier British Cemetery. *Steve Darlow*

Opposite Derek presents himself to Princess Margaret in front of the 'City of Lincoln' in 1974. *Pauline Roose.*

[Derek's evasion report:] I gave my rank and number only. I was handed over to four Germans who put me in a closed van and drove off in an Easterly direction.

[Derek's notes:] We travelled slowly that day having stops due mainly to air strikes on the convoys. The soldier in the back of the van was an Austrian, the van was stacked with radios and cases of wine and brandy, in fact I slept on top of the wine cases. The Austrian could not speak English but we managed to make ourselves understood, his main job after looking after me was look-out. If he saw an aircraft he would shout a warning, the van would pull in to the side of the road and we all took cover.

[Derek's evasion report:] We travelled for three days stopping occasionally for food. We passed through Alost and Assche and arrived at Brussels. On the way the guards told me that they had been instructed by the German officer at St. Pol to shoot me.

[Derek's notes:] We called at cafes on the way and ate bread and drank coffee, sometimes a fried egg. At one of these cafes the Austrian talked to the woman behind the counter for some time. I asked to go to the toilet and was taken round the back. I noticed the Austrian talking to two men in civilian clothes. Later the woman came across to me. She spoke a little English and told me I was being taken to Germany but if possible the Austrian was going to help me escape. She also said the soldiers were very frightened about being caught by the partisans. I also found out we were near Brussels.

That evening we parked in a built up area (which later I found was Villevord [Vilvoorde] on the outskirts of Brussels). The two soldiers in front left the transport. Later I heard shots not far away. The soldier on the back with me gave me a German army tunic to wear. We left the van and walked down a back street to a café. We entered and walked into the back where we were met by a man and woman who shook hands with me. I was then taken upstairs into a bedroom. Later I heard more shots outside.

Whether or not these shots reported the end of Derek's guards is unclear. Derek's evasion report records:

On 4 Sep we arrived at Vilvorde [sic]. The guards, one of whom was a Czech and one an Austrian, had become

Right
Derek Butcher, tasked with maintaining the last British airworthy Lancaster.
Pauline Roose.

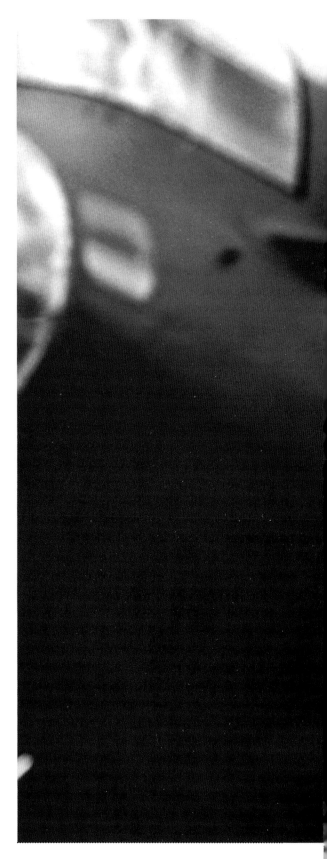

quite friendly on the journey and at Vilvorde they left me in a café in the town and continued on to Holland alone. I gave the Austrian a note to say they had done this, in case they should later be captured by the Maquis or the Allies. These men were very pleased that the war seemed about to end, and very much afraid of the Maquis and the partisan troops.

[Derek's notes:] *About an hour later a very well dressed Englishman came in and shook hands, asked my name and a few questions and then told me I would be staying in the café as the British were only a few days away and I would be quite safe here. He gave me money and told me he would keep in touch. Later the woman I had seen downstairs brought me food and drink. I slept like a log that night.*

[Derek's evasion report:] *On 5 September British troops arrived, and next day I went to Brussels and reported to the Army H.Q. I stayed each night at Vilvorde until formalities were completed. On 11 September I left for the UK by plane from Brussels.*

Shortly after the failure of Derek's Lancaster to return from the raid of Agenville his family had received the much-dreaded telegram, 'Regret to inform you …', with the resultant anxious wait for further news. Fortunately it was not for too long, a nurse having taken the time to call the family saying he was alive. When Derek got back to the family home in Ponteland, Newcastle, he threw little stones at his sister's bedroom window. She came running out the house shouting: 'It's Our Derek.'

At the end of the Second World War Derek Butcher decided to remain in the Royal Air Force. Following two years at RAF Tempsford and a brush up of his skills at RAF St Athan he worked on Lancasters at RAF Kinloss and then served with No. 88 Squadron on Sunderlands in Hong Kong. He completed seventy-two operations during the Korean War and received the Queen's Commendation. Subsequently, he flew tours with Nos 230 and 205 Squadrons, flew Lincolns at RAF Manby and Hastings at RAF Dishforth, served with No. 70 Squadron (Cyprus) and No. 36 Squadron (Colerne), and was stationed at Boscombe Down and with '1066 Squadron' at RAF Scampton. Derek passed away in 2000 at the age of seventy-six. ●

Left The Battle of Britain Memorial Flight Lancaster crew on 19 September 1976. Left to right Ken Jackson, Jack Parker, Derek Butcher, Ray Leach. *Pauline Roose.*

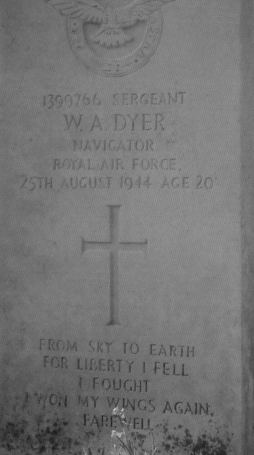

1399766 SERGEANT
W. A. DYER
NAVIGATOR
ROYAL AIR FORCE
25TH AUGUST 1944 AGE 20

FROM SKY TO EARTH
FOR LIBERTY I FELL
I FOUGHT
I WON MY WINGS AGAIN
FAREWELL

BOMBER COMMAND LOSSES ON CROSSBOW OPERATIONS
17 AUGUST 1943 TO 3 SEPTEMBER 1944

TYPE OF TARGET	AIRCRAFT LOST
PEENEMÜNDE	40
LARGE SITES	12
SKI (V1 LAUNCH) SITES	4
SUPPLY SITES	4
MODIFIED (V1 LAUNCH) SITES	44
SUPPLY DUMPS	65
FORWARD ROCKET STORAGE	5
INDUSTRIAL	76
AIRFIELDS	3
TOTAL	**253**

BOMBER COMMAND LOSSES ON CROSSBOW OPERATIONS
(EXCLUDING PEENEMÜNDE) BY AIRCRAFT TYPE

TYPE OF AIRCRAFT	NO. OF AIRCRAFT LOST	AIRCREW LOST
HALIFAX	46	322
LANCASTER	161	1,127
STIRLING	4	28
MOSQUITO	2	4
TOTAL	**213**	**1,481**

IN TOTAL, FROM ALL THE ALLIED AIR FORCES INVOLVED, 443 AIRCRAFT FAILED TO RETURN FROM CROSSBOW OPERATIONS, WITH THE LOSS OF 2,924 AIRMEN.

SOURCE: THE NATIONAL ARCHIVES AIR 14 3722

ACKNOWLEDGEMENTS AND NOTES

Chapter One

My sincere thanks go to Christopher Meese and Kevin Oliver for the information they contributed. Without their help it would not have been possible to have the wonderful photographs, letters and information only family members would know. I would also like to thank Kate Tame for her research through 'aircrewremembered.com' and Tony Capp for providing me with the contact details of Kevin Oliver in the USA.

Chapter Two and Chapter Eight

I would like to acknowledge the generous help and support given over many years by all members of the No. 617 Squadron Association. Specifically in connection with the events recorded in this book, I appreciate the assistance of Gerry Hobbs and Carol Holloway in adding to details relating to the loss of Flight Lieutenant Edward's crew originally provided by former squadron members Tom Bennett and John Pryor, sadly both of whom are no longer with us. My thanks also extend to Ian Alexander of the War Research Society for facilitating recent photography of the crew's graves.

Due recognition is also given to Olivier Housseaux, Joachim Lelongt, Jean-Marie Chappelleut and others responsible for the erection of the Rilly Memorial. Their dedication in honouring the memory of Allied aircrew ensures that such sacrifice will continue to be recognised by future generations. I am indebted to Lucy Westley, for identifying fellow officers present when she received part of Bill Reid's Lancaster on behalf of the squadron. Akin to this, I also pay tribute to all former members of No. 617 Squadron who not only continued daily to uphold the squadron's contemporary reputation for excellence, but also engaged with enthusiasm a secondary duty of preserving and promoting its illustrious history.

Chapter Three

Grateful thanks to Alain Trouplin for permission to quote from his privately circulated paper about Archie Shoebottom's experiences, and to use his photographs. Also to Henry Horscroft of the No. 44 Squadron Association.

Chapter Four

My sincere appreciation to Trevor Hordley's daughter, Christine Bailie, and to Muriel's niece Marian Evans for their assistance with this chapter and for making their family archive available.

Chapter Five

I would like to extend my gratitude and thanks to Grant Bailey and his family, and Andrew Morrison and family, who assisted in bringing the story to life and provided a number of wonderful pictures and considerable information regarding the crew. I must also thank Ken Joyce and the National Archives of Canada for supplying service records, information and pictures of the crew. Sources also used include Bill Chorley's superb *Bomber Command Losses 1944* and Martin Middlebrook and Chris Everitt's *The Bomber Command War Diaries*.

Chapter Six

I would like to recognise my friend and fellow enthusiast Mike King for once again proposing a worthy subject for this latest 'Failed to Return' volume and for his continued interest in Bomber Command and support of my work. Thanks also to fellow author Andrew MacDonald for his patience in guiding me through the National Archives of Australia and for sourcing file NAA: A9300, which allowed me more of a personal insight into Paul Sinclair's life and death.

Chapter Seven

My sincere appreciation goes to Bob Knox, the driving force behind the memorial at Freulleville, for his invaluable help and research in bringing Freddie's story to life. He's damn good company at lunch too! For source material/background about 109/582 Squadrons' heavy Oboe operations, and the reminiscences of Jeff Chapman, John Torrans and Tommy MacLachlan, I refer the reader to *Master Bombers* (Grub Street, 2008) and *The Pathfinder Companion* (Grub Street, 2012).

Chapter Nine

I would like to express my gratitude to the family of Raymond Bruegeman for their considerable assistance researching this crew. They kindly contributed many wonderful pictures and stories regarding their relative and those of others within the crew. Acknowledgement goes also to Raymond's parents, Mary and Reuben, and their extended family and Marilee Magder. I would also like to thank the family of Gerald Donovan, including Jessica Donovan, and Carl Duivenvoorden and family for their assistance. Credit must also be given to the author Ronald Hawkins for the details regarding the escape story that was published in his book *The Evader, The Story of Gerald Donovan*. In addition I am much obliged to Ken Joyce, the National Archives of Canada, and Alan Soderstrom of No. 434 Squadron Association for their aid in making the story possible. Sources also used include Bill Chorley's excellent *RAF Bomber Command Losses 1944* and Martin Middlebrook and Chris Everitt's *The Bomber Command War Diaries*.

Chapter Ten

A sincere thank you to Derek's daughter Pauline and his wife Shelagh for their help with researching this chapter and for sharing Derek's archive.

INDEX